GROUCHO MARX

Groucho Marx

The Comedy of Existence

LEE SIEGEL

Jewish Lives

Yale
UNIVERSITY
PRESS
New Haven and London

Frontispiece: Groucho Marx, ca. 1920s–1930s. Copyright © Corbis.

A portion of Chapter 1 first appeared, in somewhat different form, in the *New Yorker*. The quotation from Al Pacino that appears in Chapter 4 was first published in *Newsweek*.

Yale University Press books may be purchased in quantity for educational, business, or promotional use. For information, please e-mail sales.press@yale.edu (U.S. office) or sales@yaleup.co.uk (U.K. office).

Set in Janson oldstyle type by Integrated Publishing Solutions.
Printed in the United States of America.

Library of Congress Control Number: 2015941636
ISBN 978-0-300-17445-8 (cloth : alk. paper)

A catalogue record for this book is available from the British Library.

This paper meets the requirements of ANSI/NISO Z39.48-1992 (Permanence of Paper).

10 9 8 7 6 5 4 3 2 1

For Harper

CONTENTS

GROUCHO MARX

Introduction: A Fateful Condition

And we are here as on a darkling plain
Swept with confused alarms of struggle and flight,
Where ignorant armies clash by night.
—Matthew Arnold, "Dover Beach"

MRS. RITTENHOUSE: Captain Spalding, you stand before me as one of the bravest men of all times.
SPALDING: Alright, I'll do that.
—*Animal Crackers*

THE MARX brothers grew up at the turn of the twentieth century in Yorkville, a neighborhood on Manhattan's Upper East Side that was teeming with European immigrants. Unlike the Lower East Side, however, where the preponderance of eastern European Jews settled and created something like a parallel Jewish universe, or to a lesser extent, the Grand Concourse in the Bronx, which became home to German Jews, Yorkville was not a Jewish enclave. It was most heavily populated by Germans. The small number of Jews who settled there remained a minority, as did the roughly thirteen hundred Russian and Polish Jews who moved around this time slightly north into Harlem, which was populated mostly by Irish and Germans. Groucho would have walked out onto East 93rd Street, where the family finally settled, and heard a cacophony of German, Polish, and Russian, as well as Spanish spoken by Yorkville's growing population of Cubans. From the beginning, the Marx brothers experienced language as a fluid, shifting, arbitrary social phenomenon.

Born in October 1890, Julius Henry Marx was the third of what would be five surviving sons. A first child, named Manfred, died of tuberculosis before he reached his first birthday. Though the Marx Brothers are now synonymous with American urban Jewish humor, they followed a different trajectory from other Jewish immigrants right from the start.

The Marxes' mother, Minnie Schoenberg, met their father, Simon Marx, at a dancing school in New York where Simon was an instructor. Ambitious to immerse herself in American life, Minnie had enrolled in the school to learn the latest dance steps. She had emigrated with her parents and siblings from Germany, while Simon had come to America from Alsace-Lorraine, a part of the German Empire that was contested by Germany and France, and where a mélange of German and French dialects was spoken. The eclectic language situation at home reflected the potpourri of languages spoken in the neighborhood. The two newlyweds communicated half in German, half in English, but never in French. Simon had effectively shunned his past, which included French language and culture, and his family, about which he refused to speak. Noticing that their father had rejected the totality of his French background, his precociously contrarian sons dubbed him Frenchie.

After living briefly on the Lower East Side, Minnie and Frenchie migrated up the island and eventually moved to a three-bedroom apartment at 179 East 93rd Street, where they raised their sons. Minnie's father, Lafe, who had been a professional magician in Germany, and her mother, Fanny, who had played the harp in Lafe's magic act, both came along to live with the young couple. The brothers' "zany" cinematic worlds were not much different from their material origins. Groucho remembers their apartment like this:

> We had a crowded household in our Yorkville Shangri-La on New York's Upper East Side. In addition to five brothers—Chico, Harpo, Groucho, Gummo and Zeppo, in the order of our age—there were my mother and father, . . . my mother's father and mother, an adopted sister and a steady stream of poor relations that flowed through our house night and day.

One early biographer of the Marx Brothers, Kyle Crichton, described the apartment as a "bus station." He goes on: "The door was never locked, there was a pot of coffee forever simmering on the stove, and the neighbors wandered in and out at random." Meanwhile, Frenchie had set up his tailor shop in a small room adjacent to the kitchen. Amid the chaos, one day Minnie discovered her compulsively philandering husband in bed with one of her cousins. In front of her sons, she proceeded loudly and dramatically—she had changed her first name from Minna to Minnie, after the famous stage actress, Minne Maddern—to blame her cousin rather than her husband.

Minnie's parents, long retired from show business, performed for the children, one result being that Adolph took a fateful liking to Fanny's portable harp. When Minnie's brother Al, a famous vaudevillian known as Al Shean, came to visit, he must have felt as if he was walking into a theater. It was only natural that the brothers revered him as a kind of household god.

The death of their firstborn child seemed to send Minnie

and Frenchie into perpetual parental motion. They tended to gravitate toward the sons with the largest personalities and the greatest need for attention. Chico, a pathological gambler and thief who often pawned the family's possessions to subsidize his habit and to pay off his debts, was Minnie's favorite son. Adolph—Harpo—a quiet and dreamy child who left school at around the age of eight after being pronounced "slow" by his teachers and brutalized by some Irish-American bullies, was the apple of Frenchie's eye. Gummo, a sickly boy, also got a generous share of his parents' attention, as did Zeppo, the last of Minnie and Frenchie's children. Julius, the unassuming and seemingly unremarkable middle child, was largely lost in the familial tumult, unseen and unheard.

His route into show business had a lot to do with the fact that Minnie was a tough audience to win over. Young Julius yearned to be a doctor, but his talk of entering the medical profession fell on his mother's deaf ears. She forced him to leave school for good in the seventh grade so that he could go to work in Heppner's wig factory, in order to make up for the income his brother Chico was throwing away during his gambling sprees. Though not exactly a step toward a premed program, the wig factory was fortuitously located in New York's theater district. One night Groucho showed up at home with a box of women's wigs that he was scheduled to deliver the following morning, and he and Harpo decided to have some fun. Tearing open the box, they relieved it of its contents and spent hours delighting themselves by preening and primping before a mirror in one wig after another. Finally Harpo had the brainstorm of dressing up like a prostitute and barging in on some relatives who were playing cards in an apartment nearby. One of the relatives was a germophobe whom the other family members had dubbed Mr. Clean. Harpo went to kiss him. Chaos ensued, with Minnie, accompanied by a few other women relatives, sweeping into the room and ordering the lady-of-the-evening to leave the premises. When Harpo pulled off his wig and revealed himself, however, Minnie lavished him with praise.

Minnie's passion for performance was hardly lost on the love-starved Julius. Discovering that he had a fine singing voice, Julius used song to attract his mother's attention. If there was always a feminine undertow to the way the onscreen Groucho fluttered his eyelids and jumped into women's laps, it was because early on he acquired the character of a siren, using his voice to turn the world's eye toward him. For the first character he played, in his first vaudeville act—impersonating a German comedian—he wore one of his mother's blond wigs.

Avid for any opportunity that might showcase her sons' theatrical talents and advance their prospects, Minnie urged Julius to try out for the choir in an Episcopal church. Eager to please his mother, and feeling the bite of the show business bug, Groucho jumped at the chance. It is pleasant to think that there was once a substantial number of Episcopalians in New York who, somewhere in the deep folds of their unconscious, harbored the strains of the young Groucho Marx singing Christian hymns. In any case, one thing led to another and Julius auditioned as a boy singer for an act called the Leroy Trio. His audition successful, he quit the wig company and hit the road at the age of fifteen. He had gone from wigs to singing much as Uncle Al had become a singer by way of pressing pants.

Toward the end of his life, Groucho described his parents' household to Hector Arce, his official biographer, who also became a close friend. Arce writes that "Simon and Minnie shared one bedroom; Opie and Omie [Lafe's and Fanny's affectionate family nicknames] shared the second; the four boys [before Zeppo's arrival] shared the third, crammed like sardines in one double bed," with only a coal stove for heat. "Cots were set up all over the apartment in order to accommodate [Minnie's many cousins,] . . . who tended to use the apartment as an emergency flophouse."

Groucho lived through the spoken and written word. Overlooked as a child, he spent his adult life as both a performer and a man speaking as though he never expected to be heard. Perhaps that accounts for all those uncanny moments in the Marx Brothers' films when Groucho is outrageously insulting someone, usually Margaret Dumont, who nevertheless continues to talk with him as though nothing untoward, let alone aberrant, were happening.

Arce unwittingly suggests another reason for Groucho's feelings of inadequacy. Groucho told him that there was only one bathroom in the apartment and that household members often had to stand in line as they waited to relieve themselves. Arce adds, "Groucho early noticed that, in addition to having a more outgoing personality as well as his mother's love, nature had favored Chico in a more basic regard." Sometimes a cigar is a lot more than a cigar.

James Joyce once wrote that words were "a poor boy's arsenal." Groucho lost himself in books that he read in bookstores and borrowed from the public library. He was particularly drawn to the popular rags-to-riches tales of Horatio Alger and stories about Frank Merriwell, a character composed of almost superhuman athletic abilities.

Words that could be used to transform harsh circumstances into ideal ones became a psychological necessity. Julius had to learn how to defend himself from his highly verbal mother, who waged war on him on a psychological level. Not one to suppress her sentiments, Minnie noticed Groucho's resentment of all the attention lavished on his brothers and nicknamed him "der Eifersüchtige": the jealous one. She berated him for not having the looks or the charm of his brothers.

Strangely, in the authorized biography he wrote with Groucho's full participation, Arce accepts Minnie's harsh judgments on her third son, describing Groucho without skepticism, as if through Minnie's eyes. After approvingly writing that Harpo and Chico "were Aryan in appearance," with their "fair coloring and regular features," and reporting that after their hair began to darken, Minnie bleached it with peroxide in an effort "to keep them forever blond," Arce tells us that "some recessive genes in Simon and Minnie had combined to create" Groucho, "this Semitic child with an already prominent nose. Hopefully, his face would grow into it."

We can assume, since he collaborated with Arce on the biography, that this is the way Groucho wanted to be presented to the public. He possessed a considerable amount of self-pity, and his instant conversions of self-pity into a humor that simultaneously excoriates himself and alienates his interlocutor are like transparent anatomies of his creative process. About the strabismus, or walleye, that Groucho was born with, he tells Arce, "I had one beautiful eye. The other one was not so pretty." Arce writes: "Thinking I'd find out the medical term for his affliction, I asked him, 'What did you call it?' He snapped back, 'I called it Sam.' "

Alongside these turbulent emotions was Julius's assimilation of his mother's very own qualities. He took her hypercritical berating and turned it into a suit of armor, as well as a weapon to wield against the world. When Arce proposes to Groucho that "he apparently wasn't his mother's favorite," Groucho, according to Arce, "exploded." "My mother treated us all equally," he quotes Groucho saying. "With contempt!"

That is how Groucho treats the world. His intellect and imagination were already stocked with the quintessential American language of self-improvement and social ascent that he had absorbed from Horatio Alger and the Frank Merriwell tales. Every syllable of this official vocabulary of American optimism was a little engine of social mobility and one more block in the building of character. Confronted with the need both to repel his mother's verbal attacks and to find a language to impress her, he turned the glossary of positive American transformation on its head. He began to fall in love with reconfigured words as an antidote to the public, official, conventional language he heard all around him. If no one listened to him, then he was going to create an idiom that could not be understood. The important thing was first to attract attention. Then, having compelled people to notice him, he could proceed to hold their attention by refusing to make the slightest sense.

This was the genesis of his comical anticomical style. First he employed his body to force the world's attention to turn toward him. "I know I can get a laugh on almost any line with my eyebrows and my eyes," he once said. Having gotten the attention he was deprived of as a boy, he borrowed his mother's destructively critical way of expressing herself and used it to lash the world and disabuse people of their illusions. The optimistic, heroic tales of Horatio Alger and the invincible exploits of Frank Merriwell had taught him how language can conceal and idealize. They had taught him the intrinsic power of words. Now he would use language to expose and burst apart.

You find this twisting, inverting dynamic in *Horse Feathers*. Appearing in 1932 between *Monkey Business* and *Duck Soup*, during the Marx Brothers' most fertile period, the film takes on Groucho's lifelong bitterness at having to abandon his formal education at such a young age. This goal is accomplished by Groucho's portrayal of a college president and biology professor named Wagstaff, who eviscerates the popular reverence for higher education by trampling on the conventional respect for educated language. At one point, Professor Wagstaff delivers a lecture on biology to a class full of students. Whatever is good and miraculous about the workings of the human body becomes, in Groucho's hands, reduced to a cheap card game:

> We then come to the bloodstream. The blood rushes from the head down to the feet, gets a look at those feet, and

> rushes back to the head again. This is known as auction pinochle. Now, in studying your basic metabolism, we first listen to your hearts beat; and if your hearts beat anything but diamonds and clubs, it's because your partner is cheating, or your wife . . .

The passage gains a curious depth when we recall young Julius's ambitions to become a doctor. The card games of Groucho's youth, fanatically played by Frenchie and Chico, indolent bouts of gambling that Groucho despised, become the mechanism he uses to undercut the calling he was deprived of. In this mental house of cards, everything—his father's beloved pinochle, the profession he was forced to spurn—comes falling down.

Groucho was Horatio Alger in reverse. In the presence of riches, Groucho spent his career reducing wealth to rags.

In *The Cocoanuts*, he says, "Think of the opportunities here in Florida! Three years ago I came to Florida without a nickel in my pocket. . . . Now I've got a nickel in my pocket." In *Monkey Business*, he quips, "I've worked myself up from nothing to a state of extreme poverty." One of the handful of pieces he wrote for the *New Yorker* in the 1920s begins: "I come from common stock. I always planned to begin my autobiography with that terse statement. Now that introduction is out. Common stock made a bum out of me." Though he was referring to the recent stock market crash, the theme of riches to rags is one he mined throughout his life.

The young Julius, living in his parents' cramped, chaotic, indifferent apartment, must have felt that absolutely nothing was possible, and that absolutely everything was possible. That is to say, he must have grasped, on some level, that the domestic chaos, indifference, hostility, competition, creativity, and improvisation—the daily joy of a new adventure that he experienced in Minnie and Frenchie's household—was reality itself. And this reality was, to a great extent, created and distilled by the pressure of near-poverty. Brooks Atkinson, reviewing the stage version of *The Cocoanuts* for the *New York Times* soon after the play opened in December 1925, commented, with a sort of nasty snobbery, on Groucho's way of "twisting everything into the vulgar, unimaginative jargon of the shopkeeper." Referring to a love scene between Groucho and his romantic interest, Maggie, in the movie, Atkinson writes sneeringly that to Groucho, "the eyes of his love 'shine like the pants of a blue serge suit.'" It must never have occurred to him that Julius, the walleyed boy who became the gimlet-eyed adult, was turning his anxiety about money into a tool of the trade the way Minnie had sent her sons into show business to make her and Frenchie's living.

There is a metaphor somewhere in the story Groucho liked to tell about an encounter with one of his most illustrious peers, W. C. Fields. Fields took Groucho up to his attic, where the astonished Groucho discovered, as he later described it, "$50,000 worth of booze up there in boxes. I said 'Bill, why do you have all that whiskey up here? Don't you know prohibition is over?' 'Well,' he said, 'It may come back.'"

In the subconscious of every great comic, there is $50,000 worth of booze up there, just in case a social, political, cultural, or any other kind of prohibition—or inhibition—rears its head. Unlike Fields, however, whose character as a drunk, and therefore as a wounded man, maimed from within, made his misanthropy endearing, Groucho's form of intoxication was pure, unremitting aggression.

The terms habitually used to describe Groucho's comedy—anarchic, subversive, chaotic, surrealist, and so on—are accurate, as far as they go, but they do not capture Groucho's essential quality. They too neatly fit Groucho's comedy into intellectual categories or artistic genres. Anarchy and chaos are, after all, highly rational and calculated forms of entertainment. Those who have mastered their simulation, from Laurel and Hardy to the Three Stooges, do so as the result of a personal gift.

Groucho's comedy is not merely the product of a gift. It is, rather, the result of a condition, one that has deep roots in Jewish forms of irony and social dissent. But it is also a condition that goes back to ancient times. The Marx Brothers exist in a prolonged spasm of destruction—something on the order of rapture, frenzy, or divine madness.

This is not to say that the madness was not also highly organized. Turning themselves into three distinct presences, the brothers were able to, among other things, navigate the changing times. As talkies grew in popularity, Harpo's performance of muteness spoke to audiences who were enchanted by the new technology but still felt the draw of silent movies. Chico's and Harpo's physicality kept alive the spirit of vaudeville, where the three had cut their teeth. Groucho's puns and double entendres and sense-busting verbal explosions, even as he was drawing vitality from his brothers' pantomime and slapstick, made for a perfect bridge between stage, silent film, and movies with sound. The most verbal of the brothers, Groucho inevitably became the trio's central intelligence.

It is the teeming, restless plenty of Groucho's mind that establishes him as more than the sum of the brothers' three parts. His comic art seems to have arisen out of an intelligence that was unequal parts practical, imaginative, rational, irrational, and often bent on intellectually undermining its own existence. Sometimes it seems as if his comedy was in fact the result of a thwarted intellectual ambition. When Groucho learned that H. L. Mencken had included one of his old vaudeville routines in *The American Language*—Mencken's compendium of English, as he put it, "as spoken by the great masses of the plain people of this fair land"—he was over the moon. "Nothing I ever did as an actor thrilled me more," he said.

Though some of his most famous routines involved mocking higher education, Groucho was perhaps prouder of his literary prowess than of any of his other gifts. Early in their career, the Marx Brothers drew an elegant perplexity out of the schoolroom shtick that was a basic part of just about every vaudevillian's routine:

> GROUCHO (as the teacher): What is the shape of the world?
> HARPO (as the student): I don't know.
> GROUCHO: Well, what shape are my cufflinks?
> HARPO: Square.
> GROUCHO: Not my weekday cufflinks, the ones I wear on Sundays.
> HARPO: Oh. Round.
> GROUCHO: All right, what is the shape of the world?
> HARPO: Square on weekdays, round on Sundays.

There is a tender pathos to Harpo's answer, and although it is impossible to put your finger on it, everyone who spends Monday through Friday trying to make ends meet in a four-cornered world knows what it is.

Groucho loved the educated-sounding shtick that, all at once, mocked formal education, borrowed from it, and looked down its greasepainted nose at it. It was Groucho who began to compose the occasional newspaper column, and Groucho who contributed four humorous vignettes to the *New Yorker* when the magazine was a mere six weeks old. It was Groucho whom gifted writers like George S. Kaufman and S. J. Perelman had to reckon with when hired to compose a show or movie for the brothers. Groucho's literary ambitions underlay his comedy. The driving force behind Groucho's comic and sometimes not-so-comic aggression was his need to assert Julius Henry Marx's abandoned cultural aspirations whenever Groucho received too much attention or praise. James Thurber, in his introduction to Groucho's autobiography—significantly entitled *Groucho and Me*—pointedly notes that the four casuals Groucho published in the *New Yorker* were signed Julius H. Marx. It was

Julius who made war on Groucho's comedy. In this rarefied combat, a literary intellect was paramount.

The superficial, public contours of Groucho's life are well known and have been documented in several lives of the comedian. What I have tried to write is what you might call a biocommentary, a book that weaves the outward facts of Groucho's life into and through a story about the inward facts of Groucho's life. These inward facts are sometimes related to the spiritual evolution of Jewish humor itself, and this book is meant to tell a part of its story as well.

It is a remarkable fact that the Marx Brothers' reputation really rests on seven films, made between 1929 and 1937: *The Cocoanuts*, *Animal Crackers*, *Monkey Business*, *Horse Feathers*, *Duck Soup*, *A Night at the Opera*, and *A Day at the Races*. By the time they embarked on the six films they made after these—*Room Service*, *At the Circus*, *Go West*, *The Big Store*, *A Night in Casablanca*, and *Love Happy*—their reputation had begun to wane. These later films have their funny and inspired moments, but they are few and far between. The films are mostly tired rehashings of earlier successful routines. I concentrate on the seven timeless gems. Unlike Harpo and Chico, who were starting to slowly fade away by 1946—both did some television, and they performed together at night clubs a few times—Groucho kept his career alive by appearing as the host in *You Bet Your Life*, and I discuss that fascinating phenomenon, too.

One of the striking aspects of the biographies that have been written about Groucho is that, in the manner of books about entertainers, who Groucho really *was* is almost never an issue. Every feature of his personality, every incident in his life, is nearly always treated as something isolated from his character. As Harpo once put it, with a mordant tone that is at once phony and sincere, Groucho was "a genuine, fourteen-karat Celebrity," and the inflexible tinsel law of celebrity decrees that there shall be an absolute disconnect between what the celebrity does, thinks, or feels, and who he or she actually is. This is because celebrities are nothing actual. They are celebrities, concoctions of public relations machines and the collective imagination. They are, like the little deities that they are turned into, beings of such consequence that what they do, think, and feel has no consequences.

A dramatic example of this trivialization of renowned personalities is an anecdote that has become popular about Harpo's trip to the Soviet Union, about which nothing is known beyond what Harpo himself described of it in his autobiography, *Harpo Speaks*.

The story goes that once in Russia, Harpo told the assembled journalists that the Marx family were the distant cousins of Karl. This, according to the story, made the journalists nod their heads in approbation. Leave aside the fact that this incident does not appear in Harpo's book and is never mentioned in any primary source. Who needs sources for mythic figures? The assumption behind the anecdote is that Harpo is such a phantasmal, cuddly creature, so suffused with fun and games, that even in 1933, at the height of Stalin's terror, his presence has the slapstick effect of having no effect at all. If he wants to pull the wool over the eyes of those gullible Russians, he can. Even as they were disappearing into gulags and torture chambers, the Russian people were able to play the credulous straight man to Harpo's latest prank.

By contrast, in this biography of sorts about Groucho, I will try to show the man plain, in his full human aspect: not as someone all of whose traits can be derived from the public figure he turned himself into, but as someone who was a person before—and during the time—he became an icon.

1

Nothing Will Come of Nothing

Poetry is not a turning loose of emotion;
it is not the expression of personality,
but an escape from personality.
—T. S. Eliot

The original, even revolutionary aspect of the Marx Brothers' humor lies in the fact that there is a seamless continuity between their actual personalities and their stage personas. Decades before the Happenings of the 1960s imploded life into art, and before esoteric postmodern theories declared that life was essentially theatrical, and before present-day phenomena like reality television burst upon the scene—long before any of these developments in the culture, the Marx Brothers established an inversion that culture still has yet to catch up to. They enacted the proposition that rather than life being like art, art itself faltered and collapsed before the unique power of life lived impulsively, intuitively, heedlessly.

Their real lives never left their acts. After all, what are popularly assumed to be their stage names are in fact nicknames that they were given in real life, not on stage. In 1914, the four brothers—Groucho, Harpo, Chico, and Gummo—experienced their first success in *Home Again*, a vaudeville show in two parts that opened in New York, went on the road, and returned to New York in 1915 to play at the Palace Theatre, vaudeville's Carnegie Hall. Groucho played a wealthy man with a German accent, Harpo and Chico small-time pickpockets and con men, and Gummo the straight man. One night when they were on the road in Galesburg, Illinois, the brothers got into a poker game with Art Fischer, who excelled at delivering monologues. Taking off from a popular comic strip at the time called Sherlocko the Monk, a parody of Sherlock Holmes, Fisher conferred on each brother a nickname drawn from his real-life personality and then tacked an o onto the end of it.

Julius, who had a sour, bitter nature, became Groucho. (He was also the quartet's treasurer, storing their wages in what vaudeville actors called a "grouch bag.") Adolph, who played the harp, naturally became Harpo. Leonard the pathological womanizer Fisher dubbed Chico, pronounced "Chick-o." Milton, so the story goes, became Gummo because, as a hypochondriac, he put on waterproof sneakers, known as "gumshoes," at the first sign of rain.

Their new nicknames, which were to become their stage names, also became their names in private life, thus fusing their entertainment selves with their real selves. And they were given their new names by a monologist in the course of performing his avocation. Their revolutionary artistic destiny, which was to replace comedy with the delicious shock of men who refused to stop being their private selves in public, was permanently forged that night.

Groucho's correspondence with T. S. Eliot has always been treated by Groucho's biographers and Marx Brothers scholars as yet another antic episode in the life of an outsized cartoon character. The two men were indeed admirers of each other. But a wariness and mutual suspicion runs underneath their exchange. An examination of their encounter makes for a good introduction to Groucho's psyche, especially when you keep in mind the unity of his life and his work.

T. S. Eliot wrote Groucho Marx a fan letter in 1961, requesting a photograph of the comic actor and humorist. Groucho enthusiastically complied, sending a photograph of himself out of character, sans bushy eyebrows, glasses, and cigar, and the two continued corresponding until they finally met in June 1964, in London, when Groucho and his third wife, Eden, went to the Eliots' house for dinner. Eliot never gave a public account of what transpired that evening. Groucho, though, described the occasion in a letter written the following day to his brother Gummo.

The tension between the two men becomes palpable in an exchange they had about the two photographs of himself that Groucho eventually sent to Eliot. Eliot assures Groucho that one of them now hung on a wall in his office, "with other famous friends such as W. B. Yeats and Paul Valéry." About three and a half months later, Groucho writes to Eliot telling him that he has just read an essay about Eliot by Stephen Spender that had appeared in the *New York Times Book Review*. In it, Spender describes the portraits on the wall in Eliot's office but, says Groucho, "one name was conspicuous by its absence. I trust this was an oversight on the part of Stephen Spender."

Eliot writes back two weeks later, saying, "I think that Stephen Spender was only attempting to enumerate oil and water colour pictures and not photographs—I trust so." Could Eliot really have put a picture of Groucho up on a wall next to the two greatest poets of the twentieth century? Well, why not? Was Groucho right to be wary of being condescended to and patronized? Naturally. Was it disrespectful of him to be so touchy? Perhaps. Was Eliot's echo—"I trust so"—of Groucho's stiff, formal phrase—"I trust this was an oversight"—a deliberate dig at Groucho's affectation, or perhaps parody, of polite conversation? Maybe.

You begin to suspect that underneath their respect for each other's aura of fame, the two men felt an instinctive hostility toward the social type each one represented. Groucho was a pop-culture celebrity, a child of immigrants, an abrasive, compulsively candid Jew. Eliot was a literary mandarin, the confident product of St. Louis WASP gentry, and an elliptical Catholic royalist given to grave, decorous outbursts of antisemitism.

In 1934 Eliot published a book of lectures called *After Strange Gods*, where this passage appeared:

> The population should be homogenous; where two or more cultures exist in the same place they are likely either to be fiercely self-conscious or both to become adulterate. What is still more important is unity of religious background, and reasons of race and religion combine to make any large number of free-thinking Jews undesirable.

Groucho, who was a highly cultivated man and whose greatest regret in life—after outgrowing his childhood passion to be a doctor—was that he had become an entertainer rather than a literary man, could not have been unaware of Eliot's notorious remarks about Jews. They were loudly denounced in the *New York Times*, among other places. So even as he was basking in Eliot's admiration, he seemed to feel compelled to cause Eliot some discomfort. Eliot himself was hardly unaware, in the wake of the Holocaust, of the distress he had caused with his remarks in 1934. In his book *T. S. Eliot, Anti-Semitism, and Literary Form*, Anthony Julius writes that after the Second World War, Eliot, "while unable to break free of an anti-Semitism that had become part of the processes of his thinking, had ceased to be comfortable with his contempt for Jews."

So even as he was pleased by Groucho's grateful acknowledgment of his interest, Eliot was anxious to convince Groucho of his good faith toward Jews. ("I envy you going to Israel," he writes to the comedian in 1963, "and I wish I could go there too if the winter climate is good as I have a keen admiration for that country.") At the same time, it's possible he never lost his unease with the fact that Groucho was so unabashedly Jewish.

In 1961, when the literati were still marveling over Arthur Miller's marriage to Marilyn Monroe, and before high and low culture had so thoroughly merged, the idea of a relationship between Groucho Marx and T. S. Eliot would have been the stuff of a never-to-be-written proto-postmodernist novel. But here was Eliot, writing to Groucho to ask him to send along a different photograph from the official studio photograph Groucho first mailed. Eliot wanted one with Groucho sporting his famous mustache and holding his signature cigar. Yet Groucho waited almost two years before sending it. Perhaps the secretly aspiring literary man resented being asked for a picture of himself in the character of the comic he had become.

Though Eliot was considered the reigning poet of the English-speaking world, and Groucho his counterpart in the world of comedy, each man seemed to provoke in the other a desire to go some extra length to conceal an essential liability. Eliot seems to want Groucho to consider him a warm, ordinary guy, and not as the type of stiff, repressed person who disdained from a great height "free-thinking Jews." He can't quite bring it off; his acquired British self-deprecation stumbles into an American boorishness: "The picture of you," he writes to Groucho on the eve of Groucho's visit to London, "in the newspapers saying that . . . you have come to London to see me has greatly enhanced my credit in the neighbourhood, and particularly with the greengrocer across the street. Obviously I am now someone of importance."

Compared with the buried anxieties Eliot stirs in Groucho, though, Eliot's overstrenuous bonhomie seems like the height of social tact. The font of Groucho's and the Marx Brothers' humor was an unbridled insolence toward wealth and privilege. Born to economically struggling immigrant parents, the brothers turned the noisy tumult of their hardscrabble origins into a universal reproach to the static quality of social class. The encounter with Eliot brought out Groucho's characteristic tendency to hide his embarrassment about his origins by pushing them in his audience's face.

The Marx brothers were hypersensitive to the slightest prerogatives of power; all someone in authority had to do was raise a finger and the brothers became hysterical and abusive. "I decided what the hell," Groucho said once. "I'll give the big shots the same Groucho they saw onstage—impudent, irascible, iconoclastic." They fought with studio bosses, and alienated directors and comedy writers. S. J. Perelman found the brothers to be "megalomaniacs to a degree which is impossible to describe." There was a tremendous release in watching them utter and enact taboos in the face of power and privilege.

But underneath the truth-telling on stage there was also a tremendous insecurity, which often expressed itself through acerbic joking about sex and sexuality. In 1967 Groucho appeared on William F. Buckley Jr.'s *Firing Line*, in a remarkable episode during which an enmity between the two men sprang up almost immediately, with Groucho characteristically going on the attack the minute he perceived Buckley's air of privilege and authority.

At one point, as Buckley tried to brand Groucho a hypocrite for not voting for FDR in 1944—Groucho adored FDR, but did not think that any president deserved a fourth term—Groucho suddenly turned to the moderator and said of Buckley, "Do you know that he blushes?" He went on: "And he's constantly blushing. He's like a young girl. This is a permanent blush, I think." The Marxes' preternatural vulnerability to power or authority made them reach for the weapon of sexuality the moment they ran up against the slightest impediment to their freedom. What Antonin Artaud, with a kind of condescending credulity, once perceived as the Marx Brothers' "brimming with confidence and manifestly ready to do battle with the rest of the world" was really a manic defensiveness.

The same impulse to unman a social or cultural threat gambols across the exchange with Eliot. "Why you haven't been offered the lead in some sexy movies I can only attribute to the stupidity of casting directors," writes the movie star to the dour literary man. Recommending his new autobiography, *Memoirs of a Mangy Lover*, to Eliot, Groucho writes, "If you are in a sexy mood the night you read it, it may stimulate you beyond recognition and rekindle memories that you haven't recalled in years." Groucho concludes another letter by referring to Eliot's wife as a mere prop: "My best to you and your lovely wife, whoever she may be."

Eliot lived in one of the world's most intricately coded social environments, and it's hard not to read his reply to Groucho's rudeness as a triumph of genteel passive-aggression. Two weeks later, he writes, "My lovely wife joins me in sending you our best, but she didn't add 'whoever he may be'—she knows. It was I who introduced her in the first place to the Marx Brothers films [because she had no idea who you were] and she is now as keen a fan as I am. Not long ago we went to see a revival of 'The Marx Brothers Go West' [one of your worst films], which I had never seen before [even though it came out twenty-two years ago]. It was certainly worth it. [It was certainly not worth it, or I wouldn't declare that it was.]"

Being manhandled in feline, Bloomsbury manner was perhaps too much for Groucho to tolerate. Two weeks later, he shifts from the tack of reducing Eliot's individuality to sexual terms to reducing Eliot's social persona to Eliot's social origins.

Like the elementalness of sex, the elementalness of someone's origins was a club the Marx Brothers used to beat away social façades. In *Animal Crackers*, Chico accosts a wealthy guest named Roscoe W. Chandler at Mrs. Rittenhouse's splendid mansion and asks him whether his real name is Abe Kebibble. Nonsense, Chandler cries in faux-British tones. Chico then asks him whether he's ever been in Sing Sing. Please! Chandler says and tries to walk away. How about Joliet, says Chico. Leavenworth? I've got it, says Chico, you're from Czechoslovakia! Harpo joins them and Chico says, yes, now I remember! You're Abie the fish peddler from Czechoslovakia! And, Chico says, Abie had a birthmark somewhere. Chico and Harpo jump all over him, nearly undressing him, until they find the birthmark on his arm, at which point, "Chandler" confesses to being Abie the fish peddler from Czechoslovakia, and in a heavy Yiddish accent offers them money to keep his origins a secret.

In response to Eliot's letter about his wife's sudden awareness of the Marx Brothers and the excellence of *Go West*, Groucho, who was born Julius Henry Marx, reminds Eliot that his name is Tom, not T. S., and that "the name Tom fits many things. There was once a famous Jewish actor named Thomashevsky. [An actor like you, you Anglified, Jew-hating phony.] All male cats are named Tom—unless they have been fixed. [You get the point.]" He ends the letter still refusing to acknowledge Eliot's wife, Valerie, and reminding both of Eliot's neighborly midwestern origins in the American middle class: "My best to you and Mrs. Tom."

Groucho and Eliot had been promising to visit each other

for three years before Groucho finally came for dinner at the Eliots' in early June 1964. According to Groucho's letter to Gummo—the only known account of the dinner—Eliot was gracious and accommodating. Groucho, on the other hand, became fixated on *King Lear*, where it just so happens that the play's hero, Edgar, disguises himself as a madman named Tom.

"So I took a whack at 'King Lear,'" Groucho relates to his brother. "I said the king was an incredibly foolish old man, which God knows he *was;* and that if he'd been *my* father I would have run away from home at the age of eight—instead of waiting until I was ten."

Despite Tom Eliot's polite indifference that evening to Groucho's fevered ideas about *Lear*—"that . . . failed to bowl over the poet," Groucho writes—Groucho pushed on. Eliot "quoted a joke—one of mine—that I had long since forgotten. Now it was my turn to smile politely. I was not going to let anyone—not even the British poet from St. Louis—spoil my Literary Evening." Groucho expatiates on Lear's relationship to his daughters. "I pointed out that King Lear's opening speech was the height of idiocy. Imagine (I said) a father asking his three children: Which of you kids loves me the most? And then disowning the youngest—the sweet, honest Cordelia—because, unlike her wicked sister [*sic*], she couldn't bring herself to gush out insincere flattery. And Cordelia, mind you, had been her father's favorite!"

Finally Eliot steered the conversation toward the courtroom scene in *Duck Soup*. Groucho writes to Gummo, "Fortunately I'd forgotten every word. It was obviously the end of the Literary Evening."

During the trial in *Duck Soup* language is held over the fire of puns, double entendres, and non sequiturs until it melts into a deafening din of nonsense. (Or near-nonsense, anyway. "There's a whole lot of relephants in the circus," Chico says at one point.) In the trial scene in *King Lear*, Edgar/Tom protests the Fool's own nonsense: "The foul fiend haunts poor Tom in the voice of a nightingale." Perhaps that was Eliot's inner cry of protest at dinner, too, but Groucho seems to have missed the subtle homage Eliot made to Groucho's intellect when he invoked the courtroom scene in *Duck Soup* in a conversation about *King Lear*. Groucho could still not shake the primal shame that was the goad of his comic art, as well as the source of a self-protective egotism of nuclear force.

"Did I tell you we called him Tom?" he writes at the end of the letter to Gummo. "Possibly because that's his name. I, of course, asked him to call me Tom too, but only because I loathe the name Julius." Driven by embarrassment over his origins and lack of formal education ("I loathe the name Julius"), Groucho instinctively has to get his own back with Eliot ("We called him Tom"). What Groucho, the master of mockery and undercutting, has done is to play the Fool to Eliot, the reigning king of poetry in the English-speaking world.

The Fool is heir to that ancient heedless, reckless, destructive demonic spirit. In such a mad spasm, nothing survives; not meaning, value, or personal identity. All pretense is stripped away until the target of that rapture or frenzy stands, like Lear after his daughters have robbed him of his power and his dignity: "a poor, bare, forked animal." In Groucho's mind—at least according to the letter to Gummo—he had peeled Eliot like an apple and then cut him to the core. The strong possibility that Eliot did not share the same perception of the dinner only makes the raw psychodrama Groucho relates to his brother more striking.

"I do not want to belong to any club that will accept me as a member." You could write a whole book about that line. (I devote an entire chapter to it.) But one of its countless dimensions is the obliteration not of the self who is making the joke, but of the existential convention, as it were, of having a self, an ego, to begin with. Groucho may or may not be implying that his self-loathing is so intense he wants nothing to do with any person or organization that regards him in a flattering light. What he does seem to be doing is freeing himself from one of the timeless encumbrances to human freedom, which is vanity. In doing so, he suddenly acquires an autonomy far greater than ordinary human mortals, whose value systems are guided by the image of themselves they carry inside them.

The devastating quip leaves a fundamental question about Groucho in its wake. That question is the subject of an old anecdote. To wit: The legendary New York Jewish philosopher Morris Raphael Cohen was giving a seminar on identity at City College. One day a student came to visit him during Cohen's office hours. The student was in despair. "Professor Cohen," he said, "please help me. I've been taking your course for three months now, and I am completely confused. I've listened to you talk about identity. I've read all the texts on identity that you assigned us. I've done nothing but think about identity for day after day, week after week and, Professor Cohen, I have no idea who I am. I've lost my sense of my own identity! Professor, please help me! Please, tell me who I am!"

Cohen looks at the frantic student. "So who's doing the asking?" he says.

If Groucho abolishes his own ego in one stroke with his fabled line—never mind, for a moment, that he also establishes his superior authenticity and power—then who is doing the abolishing? Who is Groucho Marx? He seems to exist in a totally negative space, in which his freedom is synonymous with the fact that he stands for nothing. Or to quote another of his legendary lines: "Whatever it is, I'm against it."

Groucho embodies the spirit of nihilism, yet his biographers and various commentators often try to impart some positive or affirmative quality to him. His films, we are told, are either pure farce, like *Animal Crackers*, calmer comic masterpieces, like *A Night at the Opera*, or penetrating political satire, like *Duck Soup*. Martin A. Gardner, in his book *The Marx Brothers as Social Critics: Satire and Comic Nihilism in Their Films*, doesn't seem to recognize that satire, which has a moral point of view, and nihilism, which flouts morality, are two opposites that never effectively meet. "The films are a serious and biting condemnation of American culture," Gardner proclaims. Yet it is often not clear who or what is being condemned in the Marx Brothers' movies, whether it is official miscreancy and hypocrisy or high culture and people in general. Gardner writes as though he had never seen Harpo burning books in *Horse Feathers*, Groucho happily going to work for a hardened gangster in *Monkey Business*, or Groucho relentlessly humiliating Margaret Dumont's dowagers, who, for all their mildly pompous airs, are perfectly decent people.

The possibility that Groucho may be nothing more or less than hostile, aggressive, and nihilistic, negative to his very marrow, is rarely entertained. The possibility that his humor was often something more or less than funny is barely grappled with. But the truth is that Groucho was not merely, as it has become banal to say, at war with institutions and convention. What comedian worth his or her salt is not? The truth is that he was often at war with comedy itself. In his hands, comedy was just another of those official ideals that had to be deflated and dismantled. The frenzied smashing that is the Fool's métier knows no boundary.

Duck Soup is widely hallowed as a brilliant satire on fascism, and often compared to Chaplin's *The Great Dictator*. If that exhilarating movie is indeed a comic sally against totalitarian bullies, then what is one to make of the scene in which Harpo, a peanut vendor, torments and nearly drives insane a rival lemonade vendor? Aside from being Harpo's commercial competitor, the man has done nothing wrong. He is not by any means a bully. Even when he is pushed by Harpo, with the antic complicity of Chico, to the very brink of madness, his response is merely defensive. It is nowhere near as violent or cruel as the injuries the two Marx brothers are visiting upon him.

Is this scene the Marx Brothers' satire on dog-eat-dog capitalism, nestled in the comic folds of a satire on fascism and totalitarianism? That would be not just sophisticated but downright daring in the context of the rise of Hitler and Stalin. But if it is a satire on capitalist amorality, then how does one account for the brothers' gleeful triumph over their foe? Not only do they drive him out of business, but Harpo sleeps with his wife in the man's very own bed. Yet the poor cuckold is made out to be grim and humorless, and Harpo bold and glowing with vitality. Just what, and who, is being satirized? Again, it seems that what Harpo and Chico win for themselves in this escapade is an utterly negative, valueless space.

The ancient Greeks believed in the democratic necessity of what they called *parrhesia*. Simply put, the term means frank speaking. It was deployed most often on the stage, in the political satires of, for example, Aristophanes. Offstage it could have a fatal outcome, as in the case of Socrates exposing the hypocrisy and self-delusion of the Sophists, Athens's official caste of philosophers. In the Athenian theater, however, putting the truth bluntly and unsparingly could be as bracing and entertaining as it was politically ineffective.

According to some Athenian commentators at the time, Athenian society allowed its comedians to mock both "the rich, noble, and powerful people," and those in the lower classes "because of their meddlesomeness and their attempts to gain some advantage over the demos." But in that scene in *Duck Soup*, it is the meddlesome Harpo and Chico who try to gain an advantage over the pathetic, hapless vendor. They do so not by means of good old tried-and-true democratic *parrhesia*, which they reserve for the powerful ones, but by way of humiliation, physical assault, and treachery. One of the most famous scenes in a movie celebrated for its democratic virtues is actually a tour de force of undemocratic, even antidemocratic, sentiments.

The two elemental, timeless qualities of comedy are the puncturing of the big and powerful by the small and powerless, and the wholesale discrediting and exposure of the human ego. Yet the Marx Brothers frequently puncture and deflate the powerless along with the powerful, and they replace the ego flattened by their routines with their own vaunting, overbearing egos; it is never clear, or certain, that they mean to satirize their own self-inflations in the end, even when they finally turn on themselves. "I do not want to belong to any club that will accept me as a member." Is that because Groucho has contempt for any entity that finds him less than contemptible? Or is it because his ability to regard himself with unsparing objectivity places him, by virtue of such philosophical self-knowledge, above any organization that does not see that he, like all human beings, is not worthy of any type of honor or distinction? Is it because he hates himself? Or is it because he thinks himself superior to any club or group, to anything larger than his own self? Or because accepting any tribute to his ego would compromise his comic's work of discrediting the ego? Or because he has disdain for this particular club, and his self-deprecation is so exaggerated because he is sending up the insincere self-deprecatoriness that is the hallmark of "good breeding"?

Whatever that almost mythic line really means, it is not funny. It is, in fact, endlessly nihilistic and misanthropic. It goes far beyond the countless Jewish self-disparagement jokes that precede and follow it—Rodney Dangerfield's entire comic persona sprang from that quip. Perhaps the original version of Groucho's line is the joke Theodore Reik tells in his classic study *Jewish Wit:*

> Every day in a coffee house, two Jews sit and play cards. One

> day they quarrel and Moritz furiously shouts at his friend: "What kind of a guy can you be if you sit down every evening playing cards with a fellow who sits down to play cards with a guy like you!'"

Groucho's innovation is to tell the joke on himself, rather than having "Moritz" tell it. With that one stroke, the individual's basic self-esteem, which is the glue holding society together, is annihilated. The joke settles into its true lineage, its ancestor being Groucho's favorite play, *King Lear*. The play's nihilistic theme, which runs so harshly against the belief of a Judeo-Christian world—the world of the Marx Brothers and their audiences—is that, as Lear says, "Nothing can be made out of nothing." He says this to the Fool, for whom nothingness is his métier. In the play, the result of such a nihilistic world is chaos, violence, and tragedy. In the work of Groucho and his two brothers, the result is comedy sometimes so dark that it is not funny at all.

There is a great tradition of comedy that is not always funny, from Chaplin to Keaton to Groucho's true heir—not Woody Allen, who is usually named as Groucho's dauphin. Allen is simply too funny to be Groucho's direct descendant. For that, you have to go to Lenny Bruce.

Bruce quipped his most notorious line just after the assassination of JFK. The comedian wanted to say something blunt about what Jackie was really doing on the back of that car. "Jackie hauled ass," he explained. It's not funny, not by any means; it's tasteless and crass and offensive. But the slashing remark changes your perception of the world so abruptly, it cuts though false consciousness so cleanly, that it possesses the shock that gives rise to laughter even as you shake your head at its unfunny bad taste. Only a man who would not want to belong to any club that would have him as a member would say that out loud, in front of an audience. Only a man whose ego was so powerful that he could not bear to be restrained by anything, including his own ego, would court self-destruction for the utterance of a possible truth so ugly and so unbearable.

There is something about Groucho's truth-telling that is not content to be confined to the stage, that must flirt with the danger of unmediated candor, as opposed to candor performed from behind a mask.

Antonin Artaud, in a brief essay about the Marx Brothers that he wrote in 1932, saw this unfunny dimension of their work:

> We have to admit that the humour also includes a certain amount of anxiety—even tragedy—and fatality (neither happy nor unhappy but very awkward to formulate), which runs through it like the revelation of a terrible affliction across the profile of absolute beauty.

This tragic quality embedded in modern comedy is nothing new. It's why Samuel Beckett cherished Buster Keaton's sad eyes, even writing a movie for him called *Film*, and why generations of artists adored Chaplin's Little Tramp. What is new is the streak of unadulterated negativity that runs through the Marx Brothers' tragedy, a quality that is seldom made very much of. Artaud himself cannot help turning the Marx Brothers' routines into an affirmative experience. The antic ending of *Monkey Business*, he writes, is "a hymn to anarchy and full-scale revolution." Even Artaud, the inventor of the "theater of cruelty," could not accept the pure nihilism—or put it another way, the pure invigoration—of meaninglessness and nothingness in the brothers' art.

Like all performers, Groucho lived for approval, for the love of the audience, for applause. He labored over his jokes, sometimes adding a word simply to improve the cadence. He also labored over the people he carefully hired to write some of his jokes. But the applause he sought was of a most paradoxical kind. After ardently courting it, he wanted to pull the rug out from underneath it, to ruin it as soon as it began to sound like a consensus. He wanted, you might say, to hear only one hand clapping (with the other hand holding Harpo's leg).

Groucho once said that upon finding his first job in entertainment as a boy singer at the age of fifteen he felt that "for the first time in my life I wasn't a nonentity." After the Depression struck, despite his fame and wealth—he lost a fortune but quickly regained it—he could not get out of his mind encountering a once-famous vaudevillian who was now working in a cafeteria. Groucho was haunted by the specter of being a nonentity. When, in *Animal Crackers*, the assembled guests at Mrs. Rittenhouse's manor sing "Hooray for Captain Spaulding" to welcome Groucho as the conquering "explorer" returning to civilization, Groucho freezes and asks, with an anxious face, "Did someone call me schnorrer?"—a Yiddish word meaning a beggar who affects respectability. The expression of anxiety is vivid, deliberate, and pointed. But egotist that he was, Groucho could not accept being merely driven by a fear of being nothing. He had to make himself the emperor of nothing, even as he was becoming the king of everything in his realm.

2

Human, All Too Human

THERSITES: Ay, do, do; thou sodden-witted lord!
thou hast no more brain than I have in mine elbows;
an assinego may tutor thee: thou scurvy-valiant ass!
thou art here but to thrash Trojans; and thou art
bought and sold among those of any wit, like a barbarian slave. If thou use to beat me, I will begin at
thy heel, and tell what thou art by inches, thou thing
of no bowels, thou!
AJAX: You dog!
THERSITES: You scurvy lord!
—Shakespeare, *Troilus and Cressida*, act 2, scene 1

BY THE time the Marx Brothers released their first film, *The Cocoanuts*, in 1929, they had played various vaudeville circuits for about sixteen years. They triumphed in that hardscrabble world in 1915, when they broke through with *Home Again*.

Broadway was next. A revue called *I'll Say She Is!* opened at the Casino Theatre on Broadway in 1924, and was a sensation. This was followed by the smashing success of *The Cocoanuts*, which ran on Broadway for three years, from 1925 to 1928. All during this time, Groucho was publishing humorous pieces in the more literary magazines and newspapers of the day. The brothers themselves had become the darlings of the New York media, in good part because of the romantic crush on Harpo developed by Alexander Woollcott, the *New Yorker*'s powerful and powerfully connected drama critic.

But for those people who had not seen the Marx Brothers on stage, or read the more highbrow publications, the movie version of *The Cocoanuts* was their introduction to the brothers, and to Groucho—especially to Groucho. The script might have been adapted by the screenwriter Morrie Ryskind from George S. Kaufman's play, but neither the play nor the film would have come alive without Groucho's gestures and intonations and his improvised routines. So numerous were Groucho's spontaneous additions to Kaufman's script that watching the play one night from the wings, Kaufman was heard to say with wry disgust, "I may be wrong, but I think I just heard one of the original lines." He was the first of a long line of distinguished playwrights and screenwriters to despair of working with the Marxes.

In *The Cocoanuts*, Groucho plays Mr. Hammer, the owner of the shabby Hotel de Cocoanut, which is teetering on the edge of bankruptcy. The first time we see him he is running away. We see his face for a moment, and then we see his back. He has been coming down the hotel's grand staircase when a mob of bellboys confronts him asking to be paid. He immediately turns around and dashes up the stairs, the unhappy bellboys in outraged pursuit. He stops and faces them. The following exchange ensues:

> BELLBOY: We want to see you, Mr. Hammer!
> HAMMER: What's the matter? Somebody pay their bill?

BELLBOYS: We want our money!

BELLBOY: Yes, money.

HAMMER: You want your money?

BELLBOY: We wanna get paid.

HAMMER: Ohhhh! You want *my* money. Is that fair? Do I want your money? Suppose George Washington's soldiers had asked for money. Where would this country be today?

BELLBOY: But they *did* ask.

HAMMER: And where's Washington? No, my friends, no. Money will never make you happy. And happy will never make you money. That might be a wise crack but I doubt it.

BELLBOYS: We want our money!

HAMMER: I'll make you all a promise. If you'll all stick with me and work hard, we'll forget about money. Let's get together. We'll make a regular hotel out of this place. I'll put writing paper in the hotel. Next year, if you behave yourselves, I'll put in envelopes. I'm gonna put extra blankets free in all your rooms—there'll be no cover charge.

Having exchanged glances with one another during the above speech, the bellboys [or girls] seem mollified.

BELLBOYS: Hooray!

HAMMER: Think! Think of the opportunities here in Florida. Three years ago, I came to Florida without a nickel in my pocket. Now, I've got a nickel in my pocket.

BELLBOY: That's all very well, Mr. Hammer, but we haven't been paid in two weeks and we want our wages!

HAMMER: Wages? Do you want to be wage slaves, answer me that.

BELLBOYS: (*unenthusiastic*) No.

HAMMER: No, of course not. Well, what makes wage slaves? Wages! I want you to be free. Remember, there's nothing like Liberty—except Collier's and the Saturday Evening Post. Be free, my friends. One for all, and all for me, and me for you, and three for five and six for a quarter.

Released in May 1929, the film hit theaters just months before the Wall Street crash in October and the onset of the

Great Depression. Dishonest fat cats had not yet become the object of public ire, or the seeming targets of the Marx Brothers' comedy, as they were in their next film, *Animal Crackers*, which appeared in 1931. But Groucho's portrayal of Hammer found its way into just about every one of his habitations of authority in later films.

The stingy, weaselish hotel proprietor is simultaneously dishonest, greedy, wily, impoverished, and the victim of unfair treatment himself ("What's the matter? Somebody pay their bill?"); he is both oppressor and underdog. Even in his most extreme attempts to avoid paying his obligation to his employees, his wordplay subverts the very conventions upon which the idea of ownership, property, and management rests. It was that other Marx (we might as well make that weary connection now and get it over with) who once wrote that behind the French Republic's motto of "Liberty, Fraternity, Equality" was the true reality behind the French state's power: "Cavalry, Artillery, Infantry." Respectable society rests on a perfectly respectable abuse of language. But here, in the person of Mr. Hammer, capitalist proprietor and employer of at least dozens of people, is a figure of social authority ripping apart society's own verbal conventions.

The scene starts off with a predictable satire on the boss. "You want *my* money! Is that fair? Do I want your money?" That is exactly the logic of a welching employer. Even George Washington, in Hammer's eyes, was a sucker for paying his troops. But the mention of a national hero steers the exchange in a different direction. There is the arch pun of Hammer promising the bellboys no cover charge for extra blankets in their rooms. Then it is back to Washington, this time in the form of a proverbial phrase that embodies the country's Horatio Alger optimism about capitalism's magical effects on personal destiny. Hammer came to Florida without a nickel in his pocket and now—after working his fingers to the bone and shvitzing day in and day out—he has a nickel in his pocket! If he is twisting words to cheat his bellboys out of their money, then the country Washington helped found, the country one of whose basic monetary units bears Washington' image, cheated Hammer out of his dreams.

Hammer concludes his conniving spiel by associating being paid a decent wage with enslavement, identifying "Liberty" with a commercial enterprise that is interchangeable with other commercial enterprises, and associating a spirit of social mutuality with a discount on what money can buy. By the end of the scene, you have no idea whether the target of satire is the boss or his employees, capitalism or ordinary working people.

Perhaps the satiric prey is the capitalist Hammer. But he has the best and most cannily subversive lines, even as Groucho is mocking the social type Hammer is based on. Maybe it is the treatment of those on the bottom by those on top. But Hammer is suffering economically along with everyone else. It could be our national optimism, rooted in the national pursuit of the almighty buck. But by the end of the exchange, we and the bamboozled bellboys are rooting for Hammer to make good.

Satire depends for its effects on a moral framework. Swift is obliquely yet definitely mocking the callous social and political elite when he makes his modest proposal that the Irish poor eat their own children. In *The Cocoanuts,* there is no stable point, apparent or ironically concealed, from which the satire is made. Every position is invalidated, exposed to derision.

Thus was America introduced to Groucho Marx's compulsion to tell the truth, and then to undermine that truth with another one. William James once said that if a person could, for just one moment, be aware of everything that was going on around him, his consciousness would explode. In Groucho's comedy, the comedian is so hyperaware, through the extra lens of his persona/character, of the unlovely reality behind every convention of language and circumstance, that the result is sheer chaotic nothingness, saturated as it may be in rationality and honesty. But it is a naked honesty that shifts its attention by the second, operating ad hoc, as it were, and extending in random directions.

Right from the beginning of their movie career, which was really the long-gestated product of their vaudeville and Broadway careers, the Marx Brothers' comedy—if that is what it is—presents a bewilderment. It is a nihilism constructed out of countless fragments of mutually contradicting truths that amount to no stable meaning. Perhaps it could have grown only out of the many levels of incomprehension that plagued an immigrant's life, not to mention the shifting planes of language and custom in the Marx Brothers' native Yorkville.

Two years later, American audiences encountered the other side of Groucho's style of frank speaking as popular art. In *Animal Crackers*, there is no Mr. Hammer undermining his own authority. There is, instead, the indefatigably aggressive Captain Spaulding—played by Groucho—the returning hero of jungle exploration, seeming to take aim at wealth and power. As the socialite Mrs. Rittenhouse, played by the brothers' trusty foil, Margaret Dumont, warmly welcomes Spaulding, he rudely cuts her off: "I'll attend to you later." When he does turn his attention to her, he insults her: "You're one of the most beautiful women I've ever seen. And that's not saying much for you." Yet she continues her warm reception of the conquering hero. Spaulding interrupts her: "And now I'd like to say a few words." He begins to sing, "Hello, I must be going" and tries to leave the party several times during the song, only to be physically restrained by the adoring crowd around him and forced to stay. Just as at the start of *The Cocoanuts* Hammer attempts to flee from the crowd of bellboys, Spaulding tries to run away from the crowd of guests at Mrs. Rittenhouse's mansion.

Groucho does not voluntarily become insulting, aggressive, and humiliating. Rather, he turns on his hosts as a last resort, or confronts the bellboys with one inversion of meaning after another, only when he is forced to stay in a world he does not care to inhabit. His truth-telling is a reluctant recourse. He does not want to be in a world teeming with greed, mendacity, and hypocrisy; nor does he want to be in a greedy, mendacious, hypocritical world that also demands he fulfill his moral obligations to other people. But since the world will not allow him to leave, he stays in it and tells it to its face how greedy, mendacious, and hypocritical it is, and how in fact he is no different—all the worse for the world, and for him.

The truth-telling is not particularly dignified. It has less to do with the usual satirical objective of speaking "truth to power" than with a complaint about inflated valuations. Wages are servitude. Hard work is worth merely a nickel. Mrs. Rittenhouse's wealth and the high social status it has purchased may give her the illusion that she is beautiful, but Spaulding punctures that pretense right away. The crowd of guests Mrs. Rittenhouse has assembled may revere Spaulding as a hero, but he deflates that too, by complaining to the African natives who have carried him in on a litter that they are charging him too much ("$1.65 from Africa to here?! That's outrageous!").

Like the bass and the drums in a jazz trio, Harpo and Chico accompany the articulate piano of Groucho with their own distinct modes of frankness: Harpo as the unsuppressible, unsocialized, universal desire for love and gratification, sour and abusive when unsatisfied; Chico as the naked, selfish blindness at the heart of socialized language. Like Groucho, they are in flight from conventional bad behavior, or from that collection of arbitrary absurdities known as "the law." They never want to be where they find themselves. That may well have been the immigrant's creative response to finding himself in a place he wanted to be but that was nevertheless indifferent to him. But it was also a certifiably American wish for an individuality untrammeled by time or place. It recalls Emerson's "traveler, who says, Anywhere but here."

This desire not to live in the social world has as its result a phantasmal existence when the brothers are pulled back into that world. Perhaps this is why, in all the Marx Brothers' films, the people around them proceed so surreally with their routine business as the brothers insult, demean, humiliate, and even assault them. Children, too, wreak their playful chaos on a room as the adults around them converse, drink, and dine. So, for that matter, do ghosts pursue their antics, unseen and unheard by the living souls around them.

The Marx Brothers possess the ruthless candor of children and the insubstantiality of ghosts. "You're gone today and here tomorrow," quips Groucho in *Animal Crackers*. Like children, they are ruthlessly candid, and like ghosts they often seem to operate under a cloak of invisibility. For all Captain Spaulding's abusiveness toward Mrs. Rittenhouse, she still worships and adores him. For all Chico's and Harpo's attempts to rob the Rittenhouse manor and its guests blind, they are still allowed to roam the premises with impunity. Indeed, in that scene where they physically accost, insult, and threaten Roscoe Chandler, the powerful financier, Chandler continues to talk with them as if nothing untoward is happening, finally obliging them by yielding to their accusations that he is an impostor, and tearfully confessing that he is actually Abie the fish peddler, from Czechoslovakia.

Brutal honesty, obscene and abusive behavior, explicit contempt for other people—this was something entirely new in American film comedy. You won't find it in Chaplin, Keaton, Harold Lloyd, or Laurel and Hardy. More than a trace exists in the films of W. C. Fields, but Fields got as much—or more—as he gave. Later on the Marx Brothers' antisocial frenzies would be tamed, as it were, in the violent Punch and Judy slapstick of the Three Stooges, who are portrayed as mere sociopaths. But the Marx Brothers, though their behavior verged on that of the criminally insane, were rational, articulate, diabolically witty, and, in the person of Harpo, suddenly tender. It is as if their abusiveness is fomented by the ineffectualness of their rationality. When the Marx Brothers' mentality does not provoke their victims into gratifying the Marx Brothers, their frustrated mentality becomes an angry physicality. But even that has no positive consequences.

No wonder the ancient Greeks encouraged frank speaking, but only on the stage. The theatrical spectacle made it clear that bluntness on the stage had no practical consequences. That is why corrosive candor is found in Greek comedy, yet not in Greek tragedy. Frank speaking would not be funny if it were not impotent.

In Groucho's case, however, there was at least one striking instance when the arena for his frank speaking moved into real life itself; when the ancient rhetorical device took on the aspect of psychology. Groucho's lengthy series of interviews late in his life with Richard Anobile, a young journalist, illuminates the idiosyncratic engine that powered Groucho's comic art.

"Defamatory, scandalous, obscene and inflammatory." The epithets might strike you as a reviewer's apt description of the Marx Brothers comedy. However, the words are Groucho's; and he is not referring to his own work. He is characterizing, in the legal brief for a lawsuit, a book about Groucho and his brothers.

Published in 1973, when Groucho was eighty-three, *The Marx Brothers Scrapbook* is a scandal in the small world of Groucho scholarship. His biographers dismiss the book as the work of a manipulative, small-time journalist who took advantage of what they consider the aging comedian's mental decline to record Groucho's unfiltered remarks. As a result, with the exception of some slashing comments Groucho made about previous collaborators like S. J. Perelman, you won't find anything more from his exchanges with Anobile in the biographies unless you go to the *Scrapbook* itself, which has been long out of print.

This is too bad. The possibility that Richard J. Anobile, the journalist who persuaded Groucho to collaborate with him on the book, exploited Groucho is beside the point. The question is whether Groucho's astringent candor in his interviews with Anobile was caused by advancing age or the condition of compulsive truth-telling that Groucho suffered from, and thrived within, all his life. It could be that rather than causing senility, Groucho's old age freed him from the last remaining fetters of restraint. Perhaps the conversations that Anobile transcribed with Groucho's blessing—for that reason, Groucho's lawsuit was a failure—were the way the comedian talked offscreen and offstage.

In nearly every social exchange, in almost every Marx Brothers movie, there is the exposure of an asocial quality that lies beneath some convention of language or social custom. Chico's mangled uncomprehension of what someone has just said reveals the unmeaning of what passes for rational speech. The famous "Why a duck?" routine in *The Cocoanuts* seems like pure nonsense, and it is. But Chico's fantastical misprisions illumine the nonsense of what seems like the perfectly rational articulation of Mr. Hammer's fraudulent offer to sell Chico some nonexistent land.

Harpo throwing his leg up and forcing someone to hold it resonates beyond the hilarious slapstick stunt it is because the running gag (or inability-to-run gag) presents a visual revelation of at least two unrespectable meanings at once: the hidden need to use others for our gratification, and the ceaseless urge to use other people to "get a leg up."

It is also, as so much of the Marx Brothers' comedy is, an act of self-emasculating aggression. Groucho's famous line "Those are my principles, and if you don't like them, well . . . I have others" is the verbal equivalent of Harpo's leg-up. Harpo is implying that the recipient of the leg has three choices. He—or she—can get a knee in the groin or stomach. He can stand there holding the leg like an idiot. Or he can rise to Harpo's aggression and push the unmanned Harpo to the ground. In the same way, Groucho unmans himself by confessing to amoral spinelessness, even as his confession invites an amorally spineless person to make use of Groucho's own ethical malleability. The almost pathological force of the Marx Brothers' humor is that the subverter is brought down along with the subverted, which has the effect of putting the subverter on top.

With all three figures—Chico, Harpo, Groucho—an ugly, socially unspeakable human quality, lying hidden beneath social convention, is exposed. Considered in that context, Groucho's conversations with Anobile seem to be the foul rag-and-bone shop out of which grew Groucho's assaults on meaning, convention, and respectability. In Groucho's exchanges with Anobile, the unspeakable truths that lie beneath polite conversation are right there, on the surface. They are not the product of comedy routines composed by professional comedy writers or improvised before an audience or a camera. They are the essential qualities of the condition that produced the comedy. Because the condition is compulsive, woven into Groucho's nature, the comedy is not always funny.

The realities that Groucho expresses so bluntly to Anobile fall into three categories: sexuality, misanthropy, and outraged innocence. (All the conversations between Groucho and Richard Anobile in this section are quoted from *The Marx Brothers Scrapbook*.)

Sexuality first. Groucho describes his new maid: "You know I'm getting a new maid. I gotta find out if she fucks. No, not really. I have no interest in fucking. When you can't get it up, forget about it. Do you want to talk about fucking?"

At the end of this particular interview, when Anobile tells Groucho that it's time to quit for the day, Groucho says, "I know what it is, you're tired. Too much fucking last night, that's your problem. Come on, fire away!" When Anobile insists on stopping, Groucho hectors him: "You were fucking last night. You can admit it! You're tired."

Anobile: "I guess so."

Groucho: "Well, you should. When I was your age I was fucking, too. Times don't change. Fucking still goes on. Anyway I have to go to the dentist. I still have a couple of fillings for him to take care of.

"Okay, we'll quit for today. I know you're tired. Fucking can do that to you."

The Marx Brothers' films were of course rife with sexual suggestion. When Captain Spaulding proposes marriage simultaneously to Mrs. Rittenhouse and to Mrs. Whitehead, another guest at the Rittenhouse manor, he suggests that the three of them share the honeymoon together: "I wouldn't let another woman in on this. Well, maybe one or two, but no men."

Invoking sex is how Groucho reduces the social edifice to a rubble of asocial sexual impulses. That was how he vandalized propriety. It was also how he substituted the democratic power of sexuality for the socially constructed power of wealth. Throwing sex like a banana peel under respectability's sanguine gait was the Jewish comic's version of the Romantic writer using the idea of genius to undercut aristocratic birthright. But it was also a way for Groucho to pretend to an aristocratic social power himself. To proclaim sex as the secret engine pumping behind convention, and then to make your honesty about sex unrivaled, is to assume a power over convention.

Groucho may have been eighty-three when he spoke to Anobile, and his health may have been fragile, but his private remarks to his interviewer are continuous with the psychological strategies that drive his comic art.

Spaulding's implication to Mrs. Rittenhouse and Mrs. Whitehead, both very rich, that the urge to copulate indiscriminately, and without restraint, is a stronger reality than the distinguished façade of marriage somehow recalls Balzac's remark that behind every great fortune is a crime. Against sexual and economic power, and its often sordid origins, Groucho sets the defiant seaminess of his (implied) sexual potency. About forty years later, he sets the defiant seaminess of his (implied) sexual impotence against the apparent power his youthful interviewer has over him. Exploding the dirty little secret of sex outs society's dirty little secrets in general.

For what is behind Groucho's insistence that Anobile has been wearing himself out sexually is Groucho's suspicion that the journalist is doing no such thing—and if he is, then Groucho's pressure on Anobile to confess his private life would confer on the comedian the power he had over Mrs. Rittenhouse and her friend.

The octogenarian Groucho now possessed the wealth and high social status Margaret Dumont did in all her many incarnations as the brothers' foil. But because he is still Julius, he has to use his respectable social position as disreputably as he once played havoc with respectability. So just as Captain Spaulding immediately undermines his own status as heroic explorer by quibbling over the "fare" with his litter bearers, Groucho has to undermine his celebrity status by declaring his impotence. But in so doing he proves, or tries to prove, his power to fluster his interlocutor, to tire him out every bit as much as if Anobile were indeed having sex at the Olympian rate Groucho suggests.

By the end of the interview, Groucho wields the hidden reality of sex to discredit a particular social convention, a journalist interviewing a famous figure, just as he once deployed it to discredit the social conventions—marriage, hero worship, financial investment, the rituals of high society—represented by Margaret Dumont's various characters. Whereas in the past it was his capacity for sexual gratification that threw respectability into disarray, now it is his inability to fulfill himself sexually that subverts the journalistic encounter.

Groucho implies that though he may be impotent, he has the vim and vigor to continue the interview. He also insinuates that Anobile has been brought down by the very energy and sexual power that are the blessings of youth. In Groucho's eyes, Anobile cannot go on with the interview because he has been, as it were, tired out by his own potency. And, perhaps most important to a man who prized his gift for the spoken and written word even more than his talent for entertainment, Groucho can keep talking. The young journalist can't.

But the crowning touch is yet to come. Groucho refers to his impending visit to the dentist. Now the exchange acquires the character of a Jewish joke. Listen, he is saying, I myself don't have time to proceed with the interview, after all. I have to go to the dentist. So you go drill someone somewhere, and I'll go get my teeth drilled. Because you know what? Maybe I can't get it up, but I still have more energy than you do. Furthermore, unlike you, I have sharp teeth. And using my bite to remind you of your status regardless of your biological age is even better than getting laid. You'll see someday. If you're lucky.

Truth shifts by the minute in Groucho's routines on and off the stage and screen. So does the function and meaning of sex, that trusty catalyst of truth.

"I don't want to belong to any club that would have me as a member." Groucho's seeming compulsion to gain the upper hand in any situation, even by means of self-abasement, makes you wonder about the self-abasement conventionally perceived in that line. The next exchange with Anobile would seem to shatter the complacent, decades-long interpretation of Groucho's quip.

Suddenly, out of nowhere, Groucho says: "I've got to tell you something that just came to mind even though it has nothing to do with what we're talking about." He launches into an extraordinary anecdote about a man named David Geiger, who he says "lived in the same building where I was brought up on 93rd Street in New York. He was Jewish and his father ran a butter and egg store over on Third Avenue."

Groucho goes on to tell a story that, like the reference to the dentist above, takes on the contours of a Jewish joke. It is a joke that runs through time, extending for about a biblical seven years.

It seems that Geiger, the neighborhood playmate of the Marx brothers (imagine) so impressed them as, in Groucho's words, "smart and well educated" that they thought he would grow up to be "at least a Supreme Court justice." Instead he becomes a lawyer who some years later goes to see the brothers on Broadway, in *The Cocoanuts*. He sends his card, which reads "David Geiger, Attorney-at-Law," backstage to Groucho, who invites Geiger to his dressing room.

"Now at the time," Groucho relates, "we were the biggest laughing hit of Broadway but this schmuck says, 'It was all right, I guess.'" Geiger proceeds to do something incredible. Referring to a scene where Groucho jumped over some chairs, Geiger expresses his disapproval. "Julius," he says. "You're not a boy anymore and it looks ridiculous to see you jumping over chairs. Don't you think it's about time for you to quit this sort of thing and get a regular job?"

Groucho asks Geiger what he does for a living. Then he asks the attorney how much he makes. Geiger proudly replies that he earns $150 a week. "He didn't know," Groucho adds, "I was getting $1,200 a week at the time." The backstage visit ends with Geiger offering to get Groucho a job as an "apprentice" at his law firm. Groucho says he'll think about it.

Two years later, when Groucho is playing on Broadway in *Animal Crackers*, there is a knock on his dressing room door and, lo and behold, someone hands Groucho Geiger's card once again. Geiger comes backstage. Groucho asks him how much he's making now. "I'm getting $250 a week," says Geiger. By this point, Groucho informs Anobile, he himself is earning $1,500 a week. He tells Geiger that he is getting too old for show business, and that he is seriously considering letting Geiger find him a job in his law firm. "I never told him," Groucho says, "how much money I was making or what a success I was."

Four or five years after that, according to Groucho, he runs into Geiger at the Easter Parade on Fifth Avenue. Geiger is there with his two young daughters. "Julius, how are you?" asks Geiger, using Groucho's given name, as he has throughout their encounters. Groucho informs him that he is still in show business. That's too bad, Geiger replies, saying that if Groucho had taken his advice, he'd be a lawyer by now, and maybe even earning close to Geiger's salary, which is, the attorney boasts, $350 a week. "Well," Groucho tells Anobile, "by this time we had a picture contract. I was still making $1,500 a week. That's all there is to the story. I could never convince the cocksucker that I was a big success."

Groucho then goes on to conclude the epic running joke with Geiger:

"It struck me so funny that here was this schmuck, this half-assed lawyer for a crummy company, who obviously never read the papers. Here I am a big star with my name in lights over Broadway and he never knew it. And I have to go meet him again at the Easter Parade with these two gorillas walking by his side. I realized that he was such a stupid square that it would be impossible to tell him how successful I was. And at one time I thought he'd be a Supreme Court justice!

"But, Jesus, his father had great butter and eggs!

"I wonder if he's still alive. He might be. Just in case he is alive I wish you'd use this story so that cocksucker can read it!"

Groucho's epic Geiger tale belongs in a handbook of humor. So much has been written about humor as release of energy, as catharsis for anxiety, as a way to express hostile or unsocial feelings, but no theory of humor can capture the raw emotion that lies under a joke better than the story Groucho tells about Geiger. The last long outburst is the primal stuff out of which timeless punch lines are made. The negative energy, the anxiety, the inflamed ego lashing out are all there in their original state, barely refined into humor, untouched by art, unsublimated.

And just as the seeming non sequitur about the dentist in the previous exchange with Anobile has the classic form of many Marx Brothers jokes—in which the audience's expectations are completely confounded—the line about Geiger's father having great butter and eggs performs the same function. "The son is a clueless shit—but look at the father's butter and eggs!" You recall one of the immortal punch lines of Jewish humor: "But look at the world—and look at my pants!" A finely tailored pair of pants is the result of hard, disciplined work. Good butter and eggs are the emblem of hardworking decency—as is the appreciation of them. Earthy, unpretentious decency can be just as effective a weapon as sex against "respectable" hubris and solipsism. Even the rhythm of "butter and eggs" seems right out of some impeccably timed comedy routine. "Eggs and butter" does not produce the same masterful effect.

Groucho's spasm of abuse and invective hints at why his comic art has the power it does, hints at why the man with the glasses, fake bushy eyebrows, and fake mustache, with his pacing, restless gait—half bookish, half roosterish—has acquired an archetypal presence in the culture. Groucho's life and character are continuous with his theatrical performance. His "routines" on stage and screen were seamless with the rhythms of his temperament as he passed through everyday life.

The word *icon* always has the silent epithet *beloved* appended to it, but, of course, no human being lacks a dark side, and those human beings whose achievements rest on creative expression proverbially draw their art from their dark private undersides—comedians do this above all. Until he appeared on the scene, no other performer exhibited a private side to the public the way Groucho did. Groucho Marx the beloved icon is a contradiction in terms. The foundation for his beloved iconicity is his unprecedented and unsurpassed frankness, and this brutal candor was indivisibly connected to a toxic element, seething throughout the exchanges with Anobile, which was Groucho's misogyny.

There is no way around it; it recurs in and through the finest moments in the Marx Brother's films. Even Irving Thalberg, MGM's legendary head of production, who was astute enough to see how the Brothers alienated women in the movies they made for Paramount, could not control their onscreen verbal and physical assaults on women after they came to work at his studio. The boy-girl subplots run parallel to Groucho's insults to women and Harpo's mauling of them. Perhaps, ever conscious of how their stage personas grew out of their actual lives, Thalberg did not want to obstruct their psychic energy. Chico's womanizing was so compulsive that he spent the honeymoon after his first marriage in bed with another woman. (From *Animal Crackers*, Margaret Dumont: "I'm not the dummy." Chico: "Well, you could be.") Harpo, who continually assaults women throughout their films, at least enjoyed the obfuscating benefits of pantomime. He could either be chasing women or illustrating the endless aggression of the childlike id, though his punching Dumont several times in the stomach while wrestling with her in *Animal Crackers* is hard to accept as symbolic behavior.

Of the three brothers, it is Groucho whose aggression toward women is at the forefront of every film. The fury Margaret Dumont provokes in him reaches its highest point in *Duck*

Soup, when Rufus T. Firefly addresses himself to Gloria Teasdale, who has committed the mistake of making him the leader of the country of Freedonia:

> Well, that covers a lot of ground. Say, you cover a lot of ground yourself. You better beat it—I hear they're going to tear you down and put up an office building where you're standing. You can leave in a taxi. If you can't get a taxi, you can leave in a huff. If that's too soon, you can leave in a minute and a huff. You know, you haven't stopped talking since I came here? You must have been vaccinated with a phonograph needle.

Later in the same scene, they have this exchange:

> GROUCHO: Where is your husband?
> DUMONT: Why . . . he's dead.
> GROUCHO: I'll bet he's using that as an excuse.
> DUMONT: I was with him until the very end.
> GROUCHO: No wonder he passed away.
> DUMONT: I held him in my arms and kissed him.
> GROUCHO: I see. Then it was murder!

You could say that anyone who thinks Firefly would make a good leader of anything, let alone a country, deserves all the insults that could be hurled at her or him. And clearly, Gloria Teasdale is blinded to Firefly's true character by her inflated sense of her own importance and infallibility. But Groucho's insults to her have to do with her status as a woman, not as a pompous poo-bah. He begins by insulting her figure—"Say, you cover a lot of ground"—and proceeds to insult her status as wife and sexual companion to her husband.

It is one of the more unlovely facts of Jewish humor that, when it arrived on American shores, it often took women as its target. A generation of male Jewish stand-up comics made the humiliation of women a basic part of their act. Henny Youngman's famous line, "Take my wife, please!" was their war cry.

As with every other social behavior, there is a complicated psychohistorical dynamic at work. In immigrant Jewish life, the men often could not find work and submitted to their wives, who took their children's destinies in hand. This seemed to leave, on the part of the sons, a reservoir of resentment against women, some sort of unconscious backlash to a formative child's world where fathers were virtually absent and women ruled. At the same time, the women these men encountered later in life were rarely as self-sacrificing as those Jewish mothers were. That could be intolerable.

It is perhaps too easy to explain away Groucho's and his brothers' misogyny by saying that it was a feature of their epoch, a time when women were excluded from much of public life, and when their possibilities in life were severely constricted. Still, the obviousness of that historical fact makes it no less valid. Then, too, women have never fared well at the hands of male comics. And now that women have come into their own, men fare no better with women comics, from Sarah Silverman to Margaret Cho to Chelsea Handler and Amy Schumer. Comedy is the naked expression of the spectrum of psychic injury, from amusing slights to resounding blows, and few injuries hurt so much as wounds inflicted in the arena of love and lust. The Marx Brothers' misogyny can sometimes be appalling—the end of *Horse Feathers*, when all three Brothers pile onto the college widow, in a kind of gang rape, is hard to watch. But the brothers make no pretense about their hostility toward women. And it is perhaps too much to expect men who abuse, insult, and degrade anyone and everyone around them to be selective about the way they demonstrate their hostility.

There is another dimension to Groucho's misogyny. He makes certain that it is an expression of male weakness, not male strength. He may insult Margaret Dumont in every film, but he does not ultimately get the better of her, and by the movie's final moments, he is still on the lower end of the social spectrum, while she remains on top. Her cluelessness remains undamaged. And though by the end of a Marx Brothers film, Groucho may have proven himself truthful about social conventions, it is usually at the price of his own dignity. At the conclusion of his exchange with Gloria Teasdale in *Duck Soup*, Rufus T. Firefly discovers that her husband has left her a fortune. "Can't you see I'm trying to tell you I love you," he says, his eyes raised heavenward and fluttering more like an ingenue's than a male seducer's. He never consummates anything romantic or sexual with Teasdale, which is Groucho's hallmark defeat in every film. We are not allowed to forget that he is, by any social measure, a rat, and an unsuccessful rat at that. But it is his compulsion to expose his own folly along with uncovering the knavery and stupidity of everyone around him that wins us over and makes us laugh. There is a unique sort of integrity to that. Nothing redeeming or pardonable exists about Groucho's misogyny. Yet it is an honest expression of an ugly human tendency that is rarely revealed—until, you might say, it is too late—for what it is. Like arsenic in rice, the poisonous underside of Groucho's candor was an organic part of his candor.

The Geiger story is the full revelation of the arsenic in Groucho's humor. The "me" in the title Groucho gave to his autobiography, *Groucho and Me*, is there in all its naked grit. Worldwide fame and celebrity and great wealth have not assuaged the burning wound of Groucho's origins. The "me" is the impoverished child, forced to leave school and go out onto the vaudeville circuit at the age of fifteen; he is the son of a weak, ineffectual father and of a dominating and sometimes malicious mother; he is the brother of the borderline personality called Chico, who copulated indiscriminately; he is the brother of a helpless naïf named Harpo, who drifted along on the manipulative wills of other people.

Literary critic Edmund Wilson, in his essay "The Wound and the Bow," argued that a singular weakness or wound animates the particular gifts of an exceptional artist. His example was Philoctetes, the ancient Greek archer whose marksmanship was the envy of the gods, but who was afflicted by a festering, malodorous wound that would not heal. Groucho's festering wound was his ego, which was also the driving engine of his gift, one of its properties being Groucho's ability, as a comic artist, to annihilate himself along with the targets of his abuse. There was a considerable amount of masochism behind the self-annihilation, demonstrated in the Geiger story by Groucho's refusal to tell his childhood playmate how accomplished he has become, and how much money he actually makes. Groucho's will to power, to coin a phrase, was necessarily complex.

Of course, Geiger's ignorance of who Groucho Marx is strains credulity. It is also hard to believe that if Geiger was aware of Groucho's status, he would keep putting the renowned comedian on in such elaborate style. Perhaps the wily octogenarian simply made the story up. Perhaps Groucho intends the clueless Geiger to be a stand-in for Anobile himself, who apparently vexes Groucho and for whom Groucho has a casual contempt. But whatever the nature of the anecdote, it is the anecdote Groucho chooses to tell.

Either way, real or fabricated, the story provides something like a blueprint of Groucho's psyche. Other people are hell on this antic ego that is all at once incandescent and frail. The targets of obloquy at the end of the Geiger story—cocksucker, the kids like gorillas, the stupid square, and so on—are like figures trapped in a stone that someone is laboring to turn into a sculpture. The story wants desperately to be a comic routine. No wonder that so often in Groucho's films he seems to be running away from people as they approach him (and when they do restrain him from fleeing, as the waiter does in *A Night at the Opera*'s stateroom scene, Groucho stands half turned away from them, as if denying them an actual existence). For

Groucho, misanthropy is a strategy for survival. The Greeks banished Philoctetes to an island because they could not bear the stench from his wound. Groucho carried his islandness with him.

Baudelaire once said that genius was the fusion of an adult's rational will with the innocent perceptions of a child. The conspiratorial unity of the cunning Chico combined with Harpo's spontaneity is one embodiment of Baudelaire's formulation. Groucho is another. The adult Groucho himself kept the wounded child Julius burning inside him all his life. Beneath Groucho's cynicism about sex as the elemental fact of life and about the repressions of wealth and high society, and beneath his scorched and scorching ego, lay an outraged innocence that Groucho contracted as a child.

Anobile asks Groucho to recount his beginnings in show business, and Groucho tells him of starting out in vaudeville, at his imperious mother's behest, in 1905. Unlike the bouncy tone he employs in *Groucho and Me*, in which he softens the many hard edges of his early life with wry sentimentality, Groucho speaks openly of these formative years in show business. He describes the time, during his first year on the road, at the age of fifteen, when he was robbed of his money by the two older performers who ran the act he was in. The artless Anobile remarks, "You seem to have been fair game for these people." Groucho replies: "I was an innocent boy. Why, it wasn't until the following year that I got gonorrhea from a hooker in Montreal. Then I was sorry. You know what they say. Once you have gonorrhea you never get cured. Anyway, to hell with that!"

The sixteen-year-old boy, who was appearing in Montreal in what one of his biographers refers to as a "legitimate melodrama" called *The Man of Her Choice*, immediately went to see a Canadian doctor, who suppressed the symptoms of the disease. Groucho biographer Stefan Kanfer writes that the disease "resurfaced years later," but never returns to the subject. It is safe to assume that, whether the gonorrhea became inflamed again or not, the fact of having caught it haunted Groucho throughout his life. As he told his official biographer, Hector Arce, in 1978, echoing what he had told Anobile: "The first time I got laid and I got the clap. You know, once you have it, you never get over it. The vestiges of that always remain in some part of your body." Perhaps that was why he referred to himself, in the title of his second autobiography as a "mangy lover."

Groucho's childhood was not only interrupted; it was frozen in mortal injury. That was when artistic life began to look rich and promising.

3

Fathers and Sons

Art is the only way to run away
without leaving home.
—Twyla Tharp

By 1894 Cuban immigrants had begun to arrive in Yorkville. Some Cubans found work in the dozens of cigar factories that had sprung up in the neighborhood, many of these makeshift establishments operating out of small apartments. It is intriguing to imagine what the young Groucho made of these factories. No account seems to exist of how he encountered them, but they were so numerous that it's safe to assume he was aware of them to one degree or another.

We know that the business of cigar rolling had a consequential effect on one of the brothers. In his autobiography, Harpo describes the origins of what he called his "Gookie" face, in which he puffed out his cheeks, bulged and crossed his eyes, and stretched out his lower lip with his tongue. This was the expression made by a man as he rolled cigars in the front window of a cigar store on Lexington Avenue, where Frenchie liked to play cards. The hapless cigar roller was "the man who first inspired me to become an actor," writes Harpo, who says that he stood in front of the window mimicking the man's expression for fifteen or twenty minutes at a time.

But Harpo didn't assimilate the man's facial gestures to amuse himself. He turned his imitations into sidewalk routines, much to the chagrin of the man in the window, whom Harpo nicknamed Gookie.

"Gookie was forever grunting and muttering to himself," writes Harpo. "He never smiled." Harpo seems intent on punishing the man simply because the latter seemed to lead a woeful existance. A fluid, rootless, picaresque character, like his brothers, Harpo puts you in mind of André Gide's Lafcadio, who pushes another man out of a train to his death simply because the man "looked unhappy." Often "Gookie" would catch Harpo imitating him, run out of the store, and chase Harpo down the street in a rage. What Harpo found especially satisfying was making the men laugh who were playing cards and betting on horses in the store with his father. When that happened, he writes, "Gookie would get madder than ever."

"I didn't know it," Harpo continues, "but I was becoming an actor. A character was being born in front of the cigar-store window, the character who was eventually to take me a long way from the streets of the East Side."

It is not much of a leap to observe that the roots of Harpo's comedy lay in infuriating and humiliating another person. Yet by making the cigar roller's exertions his own, Harpo also went on to use his Gookie face to infuriate and humiliate all the plutocrats and upper-class figures who appear in the Marx Brothers' films. The Gookie face is a reproach to any type of stable, dignified thought or feeling. It travesties physical features that, together, make a face rational, emotional, spiritual—human. The eyes bulge and slide downward, the tongue becomes a broken anatomical part that abruptly protrudes and disfigures the mouth, the cheeks swell as if on an exposed and unattended corpse. What Harpo has done is to take the expressions caused by the cigar roller's exertions—the primal curse of laboring, the biblical "sweat of your brow"—and to somehow associate them with death itself. The Gookie face is not a comical face by any means. But its utter negativity becomes strangely liberating when Harpo's contortions appear suddenly in the midst of the presumptions and hubris of polite society. Harpo pulling that face is like a jester shaking a skull at the end of a stick. The Gookie face is too nihilistic for laughter.

It is a truism that humor springs from a wound and attempts to create a new type of strength to respond to conventional power. The Marx Brothers present a myriad of contradictory wounds, conflicting strengths, and shifting centers of power. What's intriguing about Harpo's tale of artistic development—which is also a tale of his arrested social development—is the role Frenchie played in Harpo's assimilation and humiliation of Gookie. On the surface, Harpo seems to want to please his father. He also seems to want to dominate his father's world as it exists in the back of that cigar store; he wants to attract all the attention to himself, and to break up the card game or the betting session.

Comedy by definition flouts authority. In the period when the Marx Brothers were growing up, the first authority figure was the father. But Frenchie did not possess any authority at all.

Ineffectual fathers in general could be a boon to American popular culture. Consider Marlon Brando, who dramatized his own personality in his movie roles every bit as much as Groucho did his, and who became a later generation's symbol of insolence toward authority. (Groucho, as Professor Wagstaff in *Horse Feathers:* "Whatever it is, I'm against it." Brando, as Johnny in *The Wild One*, answering a young woman who asks him what he's rebelling against: "Whaddya got?") Brando once said that without a strong director, actors revolt. Brando himself was the product of a physically abusive father who also was so weak that Brando the movie star later gave him a job sweeping his office. In the case of the Marx Brothers, who fought with so many directors that few in Hollywood were left to work with them, they ended up rebelling against the lack of anything to rebel against. The origin of such rage over the fact that no one could control them may well have been the weak and docile Frenchie, who filled them with both pity and contempt.

Here is Harpo, describing how Frenchie went about punishing him after Harpo was caught stealing from a store, as he often did:

"Frenchie would suck in his lips like he was trying to swallow his smile, frown at me, shake his head, and say, 'Boy, for what you ditt I'm going to give you. I'm going to break every bone in your botty!'" Frenchie would whisk Harpo away into the hallway of their apartment building to spare the rest of the family the impending punitive savagery. "I'm going to give you!" he would cry, shaking a broom under Harpo's chin.

But, Harpo writes, "Frenchie, gamely as he tried, could never bring himself to go any farther than shaking the broom beneath my chin. He would sigh and walk back into the flat, brushing his hands together in a gesture of triumph, so the family should see that justice had been done." In a kind of anti-punchline, Harpo adds a devastating kicker: "I couldn't have hurt more if my father had broken every bone in my body." The spectacle of his father's weakness seemed to make Harpo both side with weakness and despise it. Perhaps the Gookie face, which says that all human striving is ineffectual and absurd because being human is, ultimately, ineffectual and absurd, is the perfect emblem of antiauthority—or of a world where authority has no justification.

In *Groucho and Me,* Groucho's memory of his father is, characteristically, more aggressive than Harpo's, but no less injured. He begins by contrasting Frenchie unfavorably with his mother, Minnie, who held the family together with "maneuvers" that "were a triumph of skill, chicanery and imagination." Minnie, in fact, later became the brothers' first manager and was the person who pushed them into show business through her connection to her brother, Al Shean.

Frenchie, on the other hand, Groucho describes as "the most inept tailor that Yorkville ever produced." He goes on: "The notion that Pop was a tailor was an opinion that was held only by him," a not uncommon, self-protecting delusion among immigrant men whose difficult new lives in the new world did not correspond to the proud self-image they had brought over with them. Frenchie was, perhaps, for all his powerlessness and clueless ineffectuality, the original stuffed shirt, whose delusions were an irresistible temptation to his compulsively deflating third son. Groucho goes on to refer to his father's "sartorial monstrosities," and details some of his father's professional humiliations, one inflicted on him by Chico, who stole and pawned a pair of pants Frenchie had altered for a customer. Groucho gorges himself on Frenchie's weakness and absurdity—"He loved to laugh. Frequently he laughed at a joke he didn't understand, and after we explained it to him he would laugh all over again." Then he abruptly changes the dynamic between him and his father. After briefly discussing how important playing cards was to Frenchie, Groucho writes about his own lack of interest in gambling. "My father," he says, "was disappointed in me because card playing seemed to me a dull way to spend an evening. . . . 'Julie,' my father would say, 'until you learn to be a good pinochle player you will never be a real man.'" Groucho adds, "At that, he may have been right. I never did become a real man. But I doubt if pinochle had anything to do with it."

Then he reverses the dynamic between him and his father yet again.

Cut down by his father's emasculating comment, Julius exists on the page, weakened, diminished. Groucho comes to his aid by launching into a long story, the gist of which is that his father is, once again, defeated in a business venture. It seems that some years ago, Frenchie had made a suit for a railroad porter named Alexander Jefferson, who seemed pleased with the result. Jefferson had made some money shooting craps, and he asked Frenchie whether he had any attractive business propositions, saying that he would not be averse to investing fifty dollars.

Frenchie did indeed have his eye on an innovation that he thought would give his tailoring business a lift: an almost entirely automatic pants-pressing machine. The appliance was expensive, costing eight hundred dollars, a small fortune at the time. However, Frenchie could acquire it with one hundred dollars down, followed by monthly payments of one hundred dollars. Jefferson said that if Frenchie could come up with fifty dollars, he would provide the rest of the money for the down payment.

Possessing, according to Groucho, only thirteen dollars, Frenchie turned to Chico, the compulsive gambler and womanizer, who promptly won the necessary thirty-seven dollars to complete Frenchie's share of the deal. The machine was purchased and installed. But Frenchie was not aware that identical machines had long been a fixture of competing tailor shops in other neighborhoods. Going into his father's shop one day, Groucho finds it empty.

> In the back of the shop I found a little colored boy playing with a top. "Where is Mr. Jefferson," I asked.
>
> "Oh, Dad?" the boy answered. "He got a job as a porter again. He said Mr. Marx should run the machine."
>
> "And where is Mr. Marx?" I asked.
>
> "Mr. Marx said if anyone calls for him, he's back of the cigar store, playing pinochle."
>
> The first of the next month, the company backed up a truck and carted the magic machine away. My father went back to the tailoring business, a sadder and wiser man. No, not wiser—just sadder, for his thirteen dollars was gone forever. He might just as well have given it to Chico.

This style of outward self-abasement—"I never did become a real man"—masking an ironic, undercutting aggression whose sense of its superiority knows no bounds is, to a great degree, the style of Groucho's humor. It is always tempered—or, you might say, enriched—by sorrow, the sorrow of a young boy perplexed and oppressed by a father who often appears pathetic. A son, Chico, proves his superiority to his father by lending his father money that is the fruit of the son's "skill and chicanery"—his mother's qualities. The imagination of another son, Groucho, completes the father's defeat in the way he tells the story. Playing pinochle becomes the mark of emasculation in a father who pronounced his son not a man because of the son's lack of interest in pinochle. And in the end, it is the "colored" man, Alexander Jefferson, who emerges as a hero of generosity, prudence, responsibility, and capacity for work; this at a time when being black bore the racist stigma of laziness—a portrayal that was the product of Groucho's lifelong hatred of racism. Groucho's little parable of his father's ineffectuality is a study in the vindictive energies not merely of humor—the story is really not funny—but of the intellect. It is the hard, obverse, cerebral side of Harpo's emotional "I couldn't have hurt more if my father had broken every bone in my body."

Aside from the mention of the word *schnorrer* in *Animal Crackers*, neither Groucho nor his brothers ever made very much of their Jewishness. The words *Jew* or *Jewish* are not mentioned once in their films, which was partly a result of the Brothers' wish to reach as broad an audience as possible, and partly the result of the antisemitism that was rampant at the time, easily accommodated by the Jewish moguls who ran Hollywood and were busy creating ideal images of WASP America. Yet Groucho is virtually synonymous with Jewish humor, though most people would be at a loss to explain just what is Jewish about him. I want to come back to that, but I propose that one of the sources and essential traits of Jewish humor is a disdain for authority that is rooted in an experience of weakened, ineffectual fathers.

The weakened father seems to be a legacy that goes back to Jewish scripture itself. Judaism is, after all, the first and only religion to believe in an all-powerful male deity whose primordial qualities are rage and revenge. No mortal father can compete with such an omnipotent force. The Jewish patriarch, the ur-Jewish father, Abraham, is so cowed by Yahweh that upon Yahweh's command, he is ready to kill Isaac, his only son. Generations of male Jewish writers portrayed weak fathers in their fiction, the epitome of that figure being Kafka's father in *The Metamorphosis*, whom the son fears even as he portrays his father's ineffectuality with contempt.

The Oedipus complex, Freud's idea that sons wish unconsciously to murder their fathers and have sex with their mothers, is the product of a late-nineteenth-century central European Jewish mind—it implies not an all-powerful father who must be usurped, but a temptingly weak father whose weakness inspires an aggressive contempt. To understand Freud's concept, it is helpful to recall an incident in Freud's past that marked him for the rest of his life. Walking one day with his father along a street in Vienna, Freud watched as a group of young Austrians spat at his father, insulted him with an anti-semitic slur, and knocked his hat off his head into the muddy street. To Freud's horror, his father stepped into the mud, put his hat back on his head, and walked wordlessly on. Some critics of Freud have attributed his hatred of religion, his rejection of an omnipotent deity, to his rejection of his father.

Perhaps because Judaism has as its deity this stern father figure, one that usurps mortal fathers, it is the only Western religion whose sacred scriptures contain recurrent moments of insolent humor. I cannot think of another religion, Western or Eastern, that uses one sacred book to satirize the form of others, as does the Book of Jonah, a "prophetic" book that satirizes the great prophetic tales of Isaiah, Jeremiah, and others by creating a protagonist who, instead of taking on the vocation of prophet conferred by God, flees from his prophetic task and gets trapped in the stomach of a whale.

There are more comic moments in the Bible. In the Book of Genesis, Abraham's wife, Sarah, laughs when God tells her that she will finally conceive at the age of ninety. In the Book of Esther, as the villain Haman begs Esther to spare his life, he stumbles and falls into her bed next to her. Enter Groucho—I mean King Ahaseurus, Esther's husband. "Will he force the queen also before me in the house?" he asks with sarcastic irony. Steeped in the Marx Brothers, I can't read the hallowed passage without hearing a ribald echo out of the mists of the distant future: "Well, I hope he has better luck than I've had."

Of course, the Marx Brothers are famous for their rebellion against any type of authority. When I was in college, I walked into more than one dormitory room that had a poster of Che with his cigar on one wall, and Groucho with his on the other. But it wasn't enough for the Marx Brothers to mock and tear down emblems of authority that, ultimately, derived from the image of the father. They had to discredit the concept of fatherhood itself. They did this to an unsettling extent in *Horse Feathers* in the relationship between Professor Quincy Adams Wagstaff (Groucho) and his son Frank (Zeppo).

The Marx Brothers' legacy rests on their films, and so before we take an excursion into *Horse Feathers*, this might be a good place to comment on the extent to which they were involved in writing their films. The fact is that no one can say for sure how involved they were. After quoting contrary accounts from about a dozen writers who worked for them, as well as other people who were present on the various sets of their movies, Marx Brothers scholar Joe Adamson concludes, "So the Marx Brothers were impossible to work for and a lot of fun; they did a great deal of improvising and followed the script exactly; they were extremely crazy and were very serious men . . . and they were totally chaotic performers who did everything they were told."

Wes Gehring, as close to a bona fide Marx Brothers expert as anyone, says this about the brothers' engagement with their movies' scripts: "They were, like W. C. Fields, largely undirectable. Moreover, Groucho was often involved, though uncredited, with the writing, and later emerged as an author himself. Harpo, though not as concerned with the overall scope of the play or film as was Groucho, was generally the key 'author' for his own visual material. In addition, much of the team's classic material for both stage and screen was tinkered with daily as the Brothers either toured or tested it on the back roads of America." One thing is certain: they never uttered a line that they didn't approve of. Groucho, as the intellectual leader of the group, had the greatest influence on the scripts.

With that in mind, *Horse Feathers* comes as a revelation

of what can only be called the scorn—*irreverence* is too mild a word—that Groucho's persona had for the institution of fatherhood. It is there from the start, in *Horse Feathers'* signature song, which Groucho sings to an assembly of Huxley College's faculty and students in the film's first few minutes:

> For months before my son was born
> I used to yell from night to morn
> "Whatever it is, I'm against it!"
> And I've kept yelling
> Since I first commenced it
> "I'm against it!"

Part of the underlying clash of meanings in *Horse Feathers* is the idea represented by the two colleges in the movie: Wagstaff's Huxley College and its football rival, Darwin College. On the one hand, in the context of the Darwinian notion of survival of the fittest—or what the general public understood as a Darwinian idea—Wagstaff's general opposition to reality makes all the sense in the world. Wagstaff's oppositionism is really the fulfillment of the Darwinian ego following its path of survival and success. If standing against everything has been responsible for Wagstaff's social ascent to the leadership of Huxley College, then that is what this outrageous organism, with its large nose, round glasses, and bushy black eyebrows, must continue to pursue. In the larger context, however, of Darwinism being the way of all living things, Wagstaff is an unnatural freak of nature—a moral and biological abomination. He is the moral equivalent of a horse with feathers. He hates his own child. During a lecture Wagstaff is giving in a biology class that he has commandeered, he refers the students to a picture of a horse that suddenly appears over the blackboard, points to the horse's behind, and says, "That reminds me. I haven't seen my son all day."

At the same time, Frank, the son, is his own worst enemy.

He is in love with the "college widow" the term for a woman who lives in a college town, dates a student until he graduates, then dates another student until his matriculation, and on and on. Just as his father doesn't care about Frank, Frank is indifferent to his own biological future. He has, Wagstaff complains, been in college for twelve years.

Darwin, along with Marx and Freud, is traditionally considered one of the three modern thinkers who undermined conventional ideas of order, stability, and social hierarchy. But in *Horse Feathers*, the Marx Brothers tear apart Darwin's subversions by playing havoc with the very law of evolutionary biology itself.

This wasn't the only time Groucho upended the relationship between father and son. Two years earlier he had published a somewhat feeble attempt at literary humor, a short book called *Beds*. Toward the end of the book, he riffs on what it means to be the parent of a newborn son:

> Only too well do I know how a screaming baby can disturb a man's bed-life. I can remember those dismal days when I had to get up in the middle of the night because my infant son took a notion to yell until he was picked up.
>
> But I cured him of that habit. . . . It all came about like this. I was curled up in my little bed one September noon. . . . Suddenly I heard my son screaming and the sound saddened me. "Should I," was the question I put myself, "should I pick the brat up again and pace the floor?"
>
> I was about to answer the customary "Yes," when my manhood asserted itself. "No," I finally replied. "No! I'll scream for a while and let the brat carry *me* and see how he likes it."
>
> So I began to yell and, surely enough, the baby came and picked me up and carried me around the room until my screaming ceased. (Maybe I'm just a foolishly proud father, but it seems rather wonderful when you realize that the lad

> was scarcely ten months old and I was feeling close to a hundred.)
>
> I repeated this performance for eight successive mornings, until the neighbors complained. You see, being a pretty strong fellow who eats his roughage every evening and drinks plenty of milk, I was able to cry about twice as loud as the baby. Day after day I'd scream; the brat would crawl out of his crib, pick me up and pace the floor.

This is one step beyond the relationship between father and son in *Horse Feathers*. Here the father doesn't merely reject his son; instead, he renounces his role as provider for and protector of his son and prematurely imposes those duties on his ten-month-old. It is a perverse comic parody of the stage in life when a man's children do step forward and care for him in his aged feebleness the way he cared for them when they were young and vulnerable. Like *Horse Feathers*, Groucho's flight of fancy in *Beds* upends a Darwinian vision of life, in which organisms follow their biological destiny in the struggle and race to propagate and assure the healthy vitality of their offspring. There is something liberating about Groucho's anti-Darwinian perspective. There is something profoundly upsetting about it, too.

Only a man whose father had no power or authority at all could imagine scenarios in which the bonds between father and son are so thoroughly twisted and deranged. "I never did become a real man." With his fluttering eyelids and tendency to dress like a woman in his movies, Groucho spent his career questioning just what manhood really is. In *Beds*, he tries to force comedy out of an absurd situation in which his "manhood asserted itself" by refusing to fulfill his responsibilities toward his newborn son and, instead, making himself dependent on his child.

Though he is associated in the popular mind with a rakish seducer who cannot keep hands or eyes off any pretty woman who passes his way, Groucho's comical persona could not be farther from that image. Groucho spent his entire career dismantling his masculinity, then using his weakness to bedevil and vanquish anyone who crosses him—or who simply crosses his path. His movies are full of him suddenly speaking in falsetto, batting his eyes and nestling his head on a woman's shoulder or breast. Toward the end of *Horse Feathers*, he confronts the college widow, Connie Bailey, in her bedroom. He demands that she stop seeing his son:

> WAGSTAFF: I tell you, you're ruining that boy, you're ruining him. Did my son tell you you have beautiful eyes?
>
> CONNIE: Why, yes.
>
> WAGSTAFF: Told me that, too! Tells that to everyone he meets! Oh, I love sitting on your lap. I could sit here all day if you didn't stand up.

The overturning of the shlocky romantic melodramas of the day is bracing and hilarious, and what gives it authority—a new kind of authority—is that the parody is purchased at the price of Groucho's dignity. Ever since the wily slave of Roman comedy, comic writers have overthrown conventional power by establishing what you might call the authority of claiming no authority at all. The slave's ultimate triumphs refresh and replenish the audience because the slave, unlike the poo-bah he is thwarting and demeaning, has no power. His power is mirth, which the audience partakes of through the binding experience of shared laughter. By feminizing himself, Groucho distinguishes himself from all the abusers and bullies who hide behind official custom and convention. His son tells him that he has beautiful eyes, as though he were a woman. He is merely sitting in Connie's lap, a position from which he poses no sexual threat. Anyone who, as a young person, felt oppressed by the movies' enforcement of conventional romantic scenarios can laugh with relief at Wagstaff's overturning of them.

But Groucho does not just feminize himself—in the conventional formula of his day of what it meant to be feminine. In the brief vignette from *Beds*, he transforms himself into both ineffectual Frenchie and passive-aggressively ironic Julius. He exerts his power over his newborn son even as he implores the infant's care and protection. It is an utterly weird fantasy. Witnessing Groucho's upheavals of biology and society, you recall what Samuel Johnson said of Swift, whose "depravity of intellect took delight in revolving ideas from which almost every mind shrinks with disgust."

Groucho, the son of ineffectual Frenchie, was the typical product of a Jewish immigrant family at that time. Their professional ascent blocked by antisemitism in their native lands, their pride sapped by all the obstacles encountered in America, Jewish immigrant fathers, as we have observed, often took the backseat to their wives, whose proactive energies were galvanized by the challenges and the opportunities presented by their new environment. It is intriguing to ponder how much of the bedrock of popular American culture that was created between the 1930s and the 1950s, a style of popular art unprecedented in its inventiveness and freedom, was the product of sons who had weak or absent fathers.

In the case of the Marx Brothers, Frenchie's ineffectuality had two contrary yet simultaneous effects. It created sons who had a natural contempt for power, and sons who had a natural contempt for powerlessness. The Harpo who bedevils various authority figures in the movies also prided himself on humiliating the cigar roller on whom he based his Gookie face. As Groucho puts it in *A Night at the Opera*, when he sees the villain beating Harpo: "Hey, you big bully, what's the idea of hitting that little bully?" Recall Harpo and Chico's humiliation of the lemonade vendor in *Duck Soup*. To a great extent, the Marx Brothers were little bullies fashioned in the image of big bullies.

As the most verbal and intellectual of the three brothers, Groucho was in the vanguard of abusiveness. But as he reached the apotheosis of his swelling ego, he often punctured himself. He was both the pompous, puffed-up authority figure in Roman comedy and the deflating slave, inhabiting heroic antiheroic grotesques, who occupy positions of power—owner of a hotel, famous explorer, head of a college—only to explode themselves in the exercising of it. Or to put it another way, he was both Frenchie, comically deluded about his power and expertise as a tailor, and Julius, for whom his father's weakness and self-delusion was so painful that the only way he could endure it was by humiliating and defeating his father.

4

Groucho and Me: A Match Made in Heaven

KORNBLOW: You know I think you're the most beautiful woman in the whole world?
BEATRICE: Do you really?
KORNBLOW: No, but I don't mind lying if it'll get me somewheres.
—*A Night in Casablanca*

Art is the lie that discloses the truth.
—Pablo Picasso

PEOPLE EXPERIENCING the Marx Brothers' movies now who find themselves not laughing as much as they expected to might be relieved to read a couple of reviews of *A Night at the Opera*, which appeared in 1935. The first is from the *New York Times*. The reviewer starts off calling the movie "the loudest and funniest comedy of the Winter season." But he goes on to say that "even when their gags sound as if they were carved out of Wheeler and Woolsey with an axe, the boys continue to be rapturously mad." Wheeler and Woolsey were a venerable vaudeville act whose routines, by 1935, had become tired. The significant phrase is "rapturously mad." In other words, even when the Marx Brothers aren't funny, they have a transfixing quality that exists in place of, or beyond, laughter.

Otis Ferguson, the *New Republic*'s estimable film critic, does not so much capture this ambivalence as allow the ambivalence to capture him in an illuminating way. He writes:

> In terms of rhyme, reason, good taste, and formal plot structure *A Night at the Opera* is a sieve, a leaky ship, and caulked to the guards with hokum. . . . It seems thrown together, made up just as they went along. . . . It has more familiar faces in the way of gags and situations than a college reunion. In short, *A Night at the Opera* is a night with the Marx Brothers, who have a zest for clowning and a need to be cockeyed that are either genius or just about enough to fit them all out with numbers and a straitjacket, and who troop through all this impossible hour and a half of picture with such speed and clatter as to pin up a record for one of the most hilarious collections of bad jokes I've laughed myself nearly sick over. . . .
>
> You realize even while wiping your eyes well into the second handkerchief that it is nothing so much as a hodgepodge of skylarking and soon over. . . .
>
> They tear into it by guess and by god; their assurance, appetite, and vitality are supreme; they are both great and awful.

Great and awful; assurance, appetite, and vitality, speed, and clatter—what Ferguson seems to want to say is that the Marx Brothers' comedy lies in not being funny at all. Comedy reshuffles reality. But the Marx Brothers reshuffle reality by means of a demonic energy or vitality that is not essentially funny. The laughter comes later, after you experience the shock of seeing reality inverted outside the formulas of comedy—and when the laughter comes, it is a mixture of comic reflex, surprise, and perhaps distaste and disgust. It seems like comedy because only the form of comedy can explain it. But it could just as well be drama. It could just as well be the dramatic expression of people who do not live or conduct themselves like other people, and whose shocking "vitality" is so unprecedented that laughter is the only biological response available to you.

To make more explicit what I mean, allow me to present that bit of dialogue from *A Night in Casablanca* at the head of this chapter as though it were drama.

KORNBLOW: You know I think you're the most beautiful woman in the whole world?

BEATRICE: Do you really?

KORNBLOW: No, but I don't mind lying if it'll get me somewheres.

Beatrice winces. She laughs nervously and gazes into the distance. There is a long pause. Then she erupts.

BEATRICE (*screaming*): I don't want to stay home night after night and watch you read or listen to that damn phonograph.

KORNBLOW: Your trouble is you have nothing to do all day. You need something to tire you out when I'm working, so you'll be willing to stay home when I'm too tired to go out.

BEATRICE: I'd have something to do if you hadn't made me quit the act. I could have been a great dancer—now it's too late.

KORNBLOW: You're damn lucky you don't have to support yourself with the little talent you have.

BEATRICE: You sonofabitch.

She covers her face with her hands and runs out of the house.

Actually the lines I inserted after the dialogue from *A Night in Casablanca* come straight out of *My Life with Groucho*, published by Groucho's son Arthur in 1988. Here is the passage that I quoted from as it appears in the book. "Mother" is Ruth Johnson, Groucho's first wife, whom he married in 1920 and who divorced him in 1942, claiming "physical anguish and mental cruelty" as grounds for divorce:

> Occasionally Groucho would give in and take Mother out on the town on his own, but usually when Mother asked him, he'd have "that grippy feeling." She'd then accuse him of malingering, and they'd have another big fight—very often at the dinner table in front of Miriam [Arthur's little sister] and me—and she'd storm out of the house.
>
> "I don't want to stay home night after night and watch you read or listen to that damn phonograph," Mother would scream.
>
> "Your trouble is you have nothing to do all day," he'd point out calmly.
>
> "You need something to tire you out when I'm working, so you'll be willing to stay home when I'm too tired to go out."
>
> "I'd have something to do if you hadn't made me quit the act," she'd reply. "I could have been a great dancer—now it's too late."
>
> This would generally evoke a peal of derisive laughter from Groucho, who would tell her that she was damn lucky she didn't have to support herself with the little talent she had.
>
> Following a crack like that she'd generally call him a son of a bitch, and run out of the house again.

I am not trying to reduce Groucho's comic art to a personality flaw. His treatment of Ruth was perhaps a typical manifestation of that almost helpless misogyny of his. What I want to try to show is to what extent the Marx Brothers, every bit as Oscar Wilde did on a different level, dissolved the boundary between life and art, public and private.

Picasso's bon mot about art being the lie that discloses the truth seems to me a mistaken notion. Art doesn't lie. It creates an imaginary or hypothetical situation, but that is not the same thing as a lie, which directly contradicts a provable fact. It is not a lie to tell a story about a Danish prince who cannot decide whether to exact revenge after his father's ghost tells him that he was murdered by his brother. It is a lie to say that Hamlet was written by Sid Caesar. A more accurate, if less striking, way to put it would be to say that art is a parallel world that reveals the truth of our familiar world.

Popular art has had a different function. Popular art is the lie that obscures the truth. It makes our days easier to bear. Oscar Wilde once quipped that the basis of optimism is sheer terror, and it is the terror of reality, of suffering and death, that we seek to escape when we pick up a detective novel, with its tidy endings, or go to see a Hollywood movie, which, for all contemporary films' graphic portrayals of just about everything, still presents us with optimistic closures.

The Marx Brothers turned the contrasting roles of high art and popular art on their heads. Like Chaplin, the Marx Brothers used popular art to convey truth once confined to the rarefied precincts of high culture, especially in the realm of comedy. Unlike Chaplin, they burst the form of popular art in the course of doing so. Ever since Lenny Bruce made his dark non-joke about Jackie "hauling ass," we have become accustomed to one comedian after another—Sam Kinison, Richard Pryor, Robin Williams, Margaret Cho, Sarah Silverman, Jon Stewart, Stephen Colbert, Lewis Black—uttering the unutterable. With the exception of Bruce, whose nightclub act failed to attain the reach that the Marx Brothers did with their style of frank, brute intensity, there has never been a comedian who so uncompromisingly substituted raw, shocking truthfulness for humor. The Marx Brothers' audiences laughed, not only because they were tickled and delighted, but because the scales fell helter-skelter from their eyes. There are slapstick routines and out-and-out jokes, to be sure, but so much of the Marx Brothers' humor consists of simply saying or doing something in a social situation that is true to the social and psychological dynamics of the situation, but which no one would ever say or do in public.

What is hard to realize when watching the films is that the Brothers were not merely acting, but living. For all their fastidiousness about lines and timing—Groucho would notoriously throw out one perfectly good scene after another because they did not meet his anxious standards—they existed in their films the way they conducted themselves in ordinary life.

Arthur Marx, in his memoir, *My Life with Groucho,* recalls what it was like to be at the dinner table with his father and his three famous uncles:

> They were loud, raucous, and never took anything seriously. The jokes would fly back and forth across the table so rapidly you couldn't keep up with them. And all the brothers but my father were accomplished at the art of doing table tricks. They'd be springboarding silverware into glasses of water, making rabbits out of napkins, pulling cards from their sleeves, and perhaps shooting dice with sugar cubes.

"Groucho never knew how to talk normally," said the actress Maureen O'Sullivan, who appeared in *A Day at the Races,* and whom Groucho unsuccessfully tried to seduce offscreen. "After a while," she said about his rapid-fire patter, "your face starts to crack." Asked whether Groucho's screen persona was like his actual personality, Susan Marx, Harpo's wife, replied: "You bet your life it is!"

In the mid-1930s, when the Brothers' career was at a turning point and they left Paramount Pictures for MGM, anxious that their low-earning previous picture, a semiflop called *Duck Soup,* had spelled the end of their careers, they found themselves in the anteroom to Irving Thalberg's office. Thalberg was as feared as he was famously difficult to see, and he kept the nervous brothers waiting for hours. Finally they each lit up a cigar and began to blow smoke under Thalberg's door, shouting "Fire!" The next time they went to see him he ushered them into his office right away, but then kept them waiting for hours while he went down the hall to the office of Louis B. Mayer, the studio head. When Thalberg returned, he found the brothers sitting naked before a crackling fire in his fireplace, roasting potatoes.

In the late 1920s, Groucho moved to Great Neck, Long Island, buying a ten-room, two-story stucco house equipped with a special bluestone gravel driveway where he could park his beloved Lincoln. At the time, Great Neck was home to many illustrious entertainment figures, such as George M. Cohan, Oscar Hammerstein II, and Eddie Cantor, as well as the likes of P. G. Wodehouse and Eugene O'Neill (whom Groucho enjoyed mercilessly parodying in his films). In 1931, Groucho gave up his Great Neck home to bring his long-suffering first wife, Ruth, and their two children, twelve-year-old Arthur and his little sister, Miriam, to Hollywood in order to join Groucho's brothers there. Before that, however, he took the family on a trip to Europe, along with his brothers, of course—they seemed never to go anywhere without each other. Arriving back in New York, Groucho became exasperated with the official process of reentering the country through customs. He filled out the declaration of purchases form without, one might say, breaking character:

> Name: Julius H. Marx
> Address: 21 Lincoln Rd., Great Neck, Long Island
> Born: Yes
> Hair: Not much
> Eyes: All the better to see you with
> Occupation: Smuggler
> List of Items Purchased Out of the United States, Where Bought, and the Purchase Price: Wouldn't you like to know?

After filling out the form, Groucho turned to his wife, Ruth, in front of the customs officials, and asked her whether she was still carrying the opium. The customs agents grabbed Groucho, Ruth, and their two small children. They took the family into a room, made them all strip naked, and examined them for hidden goods. Then they had the family wait, presumably clothed once again, for hours while the officials meticulously searched their luggage.

Such incidents are revered episodes in the biographical lore surrounding the Marxes' lives. They are presented merrily, as yet more examples of the Brothers' spirit of liberating freedom and anarchy. This misses their dark side. To be sure, by the time the incidents I've recounted took place, Groucho and his brothers had become world famous for being abusive toward respectability and authority. But they were as much the passive victims of destructive temperaments as the artistically triumphant products of same. There is nothing funny about two small children being strip-searched and forced to watch their parents undergo the same humiliating process.

Groucho's dark, compulsive assault not just on propriety but on the basic premises of social life is what makes the Marx Brothers' movies so strange, and so original. The humor, as I've noted, is often not humor. It is the spectacle of seeing something so uncivilized and natural that it has all the appearance of a freakish exception to human nature. It is like watching a wild animal that does not know it is being watched. It is the acting style of people who are not really acting.

The most unforgettable acting is the product of untethered, otherworldly, orphan personalities who are chosen by acting rather than the other way around. They fall helplessly through the social cracks and tumble into their vocation. Louis Malle expresses this superbly at the beginning of *Uncle Vanya on 42nd Street*. We see the actors coming in off the street, talking to one another as themselves, changing into their costumes as themselves, and then, imperceptibly, seamlessly, becoming the characters they are playing.

The same transformation takes place in Al Pacino's film about playing Richard III, *Looking for Richard*. At one point, we see Pacino at the Cloisters, New York City's museum of medieval art. Pacino is walking outside, through a colonnade. He is wearing a gorgeous overcoat, which recalls the lush overcoat Marlon Brando wore in *Last Tango in Paris*, another movie about the blurred lines between living and acting that interweaves Brando's life story with that of his character in that film. One minute Pacino is talking as Pacino. Then he does a kind of pirouette and, while still talking and walking as Pacino, becomes Shakespeare's hunchbacked king.

Though Groucho and his brothers are hardly ever regarded as actors, they possessed a great actor's inborn vulnerability to his or her eventual calling. The similarity to Pacino in this respect is striking. Like them, he grew up virtually parentless, in a crowded tenement where he was often lost in the crowd. Pretense became an almost biological necessity. The young Pacino was always one step away from pretending to be someone else as a means to fulfilling who he really was. I once wrote a profile of him for a magazine, and he held me rapt over the phone late one night as he described the Louis Malle–like moment when the cast of *The Godfather* met for the first time at an Italian restaurant in East Harlem. By the end of the dinner, Pacino said, Brando

> was responding to me without knowing me, as if I was that kid, who was not quite decided as to what he wanted to do, and that, somehow, as his son, I had something that Marlon wanted to cultivate, and that he was sensitive to in his youngest son.

What Pacino, who had been abandoned by his father when he was two, didn't say was that it was he who had responded to Brando as his father.

Groucho and his brothers also had what you might call a natural richness born of deficiency. They drifted, simultaneously, into their stage personas and the completion of their development—or lack thereof—as people. Though young Julius had his heart set on becoming a doctor, his marginal position in his parents' household and his compensatory passion for words drew him helplessly toward the world of entertainment. His ideal and the model that he based both his stage persona and his personality on was his uncle Al Shean, the famous vaudevillian. In *Groucho and Me*, Groucho describes Shean's appearances at 179 East 93rd Street:

> I have now told you about three uncles who were all nice fellows, but miserable failures in their respective careers. [This tally does not include his devastating portrait of his father, the failed tailor.] I might as well confess all and tell you that I also had an uncle who was a great success. He was my mother's brother. His name was Shean, and with a partner named Gallagher, he sang a song ["Mr. Gallagher and Mr. Shean"] that, today, is as much a part of America as baseball.

He goes on to talk about how Shean had been a pants presser in a New York City sweatshop. Shean had a beautiful voice, Groucho relates, and he organized a quartet in the shop, who sang while they worked, with the result that they got themselves fired. That impelled Shean to enter show business. Groucho continues:

> Originally, I wanted to be a doctor. But my uncle Al's success convinced my mother that the theater was a soft and lucrative racket, and that I had better forget about the Hippocratic oath. . . . My uncle Al was a handsome dog, and when he came to visit us things started moving. We were all rushed

> to different stores to buy the foods he liked. . . . At the end of the meal, each of the boys got a buck from Uncle Al. Since my allowance was only a nickel a week, this gift of a dollar meant luxury for many weeks. . . .
>
> When my uncle came to visit us he had long hair down his neck, pre-Presley sideburns, a frock coat, a gold-headed cane and a silk hat. . . . By the time Uncle Al left the house, there would be quite a crowd hanging around the front stoop. On leaving, he would toss a handful of nickels in the air and watch the kids scramble for them.
>
> Here was glamour!

And here was Julius's vocation in the form of a familiar family routine. Think of the characters Groucho plays, and of the way they make their entrance. In *Cocoanuts* Hammer is immediately surrounded by a crowd of bellboys, who are dependent on him for their livelihood. A wealthy, privileged crowd of admirers jubilantly greets Groucho when, in *Animal Crackers*, he makes his entrance as the celebrated explorer Captain Spaulding. In *Horse Feathers*, Professor Wagstaff is introduced to a quiet and respectful faculty as the new president of Huxley College. In *Duck Soup*, Groucho, as Rufus T. Firefly, becomes leader of the country of Freedonia just minutes into the film. In *A Night at the Opera*, Margaret Dumont plays a wealthy patron of the arts around whom various important suitors, including the head of the Metropolitan Opera, hungrily orbit. When the film begins, she is waiting in a restaurant for Groucho's Otis Driftwood, a sort of freelance impresario, who is horribly late. Nevertheless, he has her in his thrall. In *A Day at the Races*, Hugo Z. Hackenbush is the only means of salvation for the struggling Standish Sanitarium. His arrival is greeted with celebration and relief—despite the fact that, unbeknownst to the celebrants, he is actually a veterinarian.

Each of these characters makes his entrance as a larger-than-life figure, absurdly idealized or romanticized, or at least inflated, by the inhabitants of his social milieu. In every case, Groucho is reenacting Uncle Al's sudden dramatic appearances at the Marxes' household. Just as Uncle Al's glamour lay in the fact that he was an actor who made his living playing fictional characters, Groucho's fictional character is always pretending to be someone he is not. Since Julius's persona as Groucho was really who Julius was, the circle is complete. Uncle Al the actor finds his continuation in Julius playing Groucho impersonating a grand figure who has the same stature Uncle Al once enjoyed at the Marxes'.

To make things even more confusing—and clarifying at the same time—Groucho's characters all exist right on the cusp of making some kind of fortune. They first appear to the fictional world around them as successful, prosperous figures who are expected, at any moment, to shower those around them with coins. Here was glamour! A glamour every bit as impressive as Uncle Al himself tossing a handful of nickels in the air to the neighborhood kids.

Interlude: Words

For I am a Pirate King!
And it is, it is a glorious thing
To be a Pirate King!
—*Pirates of Penzance*

You might imagine the verbal young Julius talking and talking. No one listens to him. And so, in the manner of someone whose words go ignored, he begins to speak more and more outrageously, until everyone turns toward him.

Groucho loved the long stream of doggerel patter that often closed a vaudeville act. By around 1907, Minnie had satisfied herself that all her children with the exception of the youngest, Zeppo, were finished with their formal schooling, and she took them out on the vaudeville circuit, in 1916 moving the whole family to Chicago, where she worked as a small-time booking agent, representing mostly the Brothers. The Brothers began as the Nightingales, sometimes Three Nightingales—Julius and Milton (Gummo) and two other non–family members, who alternated from performance to performance—eventually becoming Four Nightingales once Harpo joined the act.

Their first real routine was a variation on vaudeville's venerable old schoolroom shtick. They called it Fun in Hi Skule. It was no wonder the routine was, for a time, a smashing success. School had offered these ambitious immigrant children a way up and out of their impoverished circumstances. Leaving it was a special kind of anguish—and also a special kind of liberation—and the Brothers characteristically threw themselves into mocking and obliterating the one experience that might have guaranteed them a stable life.

Fun in Hi Skule was an efficient conversion of childhood wounds into adult vengeance. As one Marxian scholar puts it, "Harpo blacked out some teeth, put on a ratty red wig, and stuck a sand bucket over his head and he was Patsy Brannigan, the standard bumpkin. Groucho put on a German accent and became Mr. Green, the customary angry teacher." That is to say, Harpo both became and comically obliterated the pair of Irish bullies who tormented him and literally threw him out of elementary school—they tossed him out of a second-floor window again and again. Groucho turned himself into the type of learned figure he emulated, and filled that figure up with the anger he felt over, among many other things, having to end his education in the seventh grade. Mr. Green also had a German accent, which gave Julius the opportunity to mock the way Minnie's parents—Minnie, his eternal persecutor and eternal patron—spoke.

As was true of most vaudeville acts, Fun in Hi Skule's routines reflected its audience's everyday experience, and gave these experiences absurd little twists that lifted them out of the realm of the mundane into surprise, and thus comedy:

GROUCHO: Why were you late?

HARPO: My mother lost the lid off the stove, and I had to sit on it to keep the smoke in.

GROUCHO: If you had ten apples and you wanted to divide them among six people, what would you do?

HARPO: Make applesauce.

It is almost inevitable that the act closed in doggerel, where words blur and melt and lose their conventional meaning. In doggerel, words are reborn into a world where their meaning is defined by how they sound, how they sound alongside other words, and how funny the result is when the conventional meaning of all the words gets knocked around and inverted. Al Shean, who had taken the Brothers' careers in hand and often wrote their material, paid either twenty-five, twenty-seven, or fifty dollars to a man named Charley Van for the doggerel that closed Fun in Hi Skule. They called it "Peasie Weasie." Some of the verses went like this:

My mother called Sister downstairs the other day.
"I'm taking a bath," my sister did say.
"Well, slip on something quick; here comes Mr. Brown."
She slipped on the top step and then came down.

Peasie Weasie, that's his name.
Peasie Weasie, Peasie Weasie what's his game?
He will catch you if he can,
Peasie Weasie, Peasie Weasie is a bold, bad man.

A humpback went to see a football game,
The game was called on account of rain.
The humpback asked the halfback for his quarter back,
And the fullback kicked the hump off the humpback's back.

Went fishing last Sunday and caught a smelt,
Put him in the fire and the fire he felt,
Of all the smelts I ever smelt,
I never smelt a smelt like that smelt smelt.

Within this new verbal world, words become reconstituted as free, autonomous entities, no longer bound to their conventional, social meanings. The new, reconstituted words throw open new horizons of meaning, a revelation not lost on three men who were once poor and oppressed by seeming immovable social givens. Peasie-Weasie patter is asocial, and only one step away from lying outside the boundaries of what is proper to say: "And the fullback kicked the hump off the humpback's back."

Once again, the image of the young child comes to mind, someone who is used to never being heard. He talks and talks, but only the louder, better-looking, and more charming other children or siblings are paid attention to. So he sits off to the side, bending and breaking the vessels of conventional meaning that words are, because the social conventions have betrayed him. "Mom, the cat ran out the door! Mom! The cat ran away! Mom, the cat ran out of the house! Mom! The house is on fire! Mom, I'm dying, my stomach is killing me, I'm going to be dead. Mom! Mom, the kitchen is on fire! Mom! I never smelt a smelt like that smelt smelt!"

There are two ways to both attract attention and outrage the conventions that have denied you that attention. One is to use language to shock. The other is to use the body to shock. One, in other words, is intellectual. The other is visceral.

Groucho, the neglected introvert, who loved books, naturally chose the verbal route. For all his subversions achieved by means of contorting logic, he was supremely rational. In splintering the meaning of words, he imbued them with new sense, a new rationality: a suprarationality, if you will. A higher sense of meaning and order existing above conventional meaning is akin to music, for music, based on mathematical relationships, is nothing if not a higher rationality. Groucho loved "Peasie Weasie" all his life, and, on a different level and in a different register, revered the lyrics of Gilbert and Sullivan. He loved the freedom that ensued after the reconfiguration of conventional language.

But for all his aspirations to high culture, he was not as stately and refined as the English duo. His assaults on respectable language—language that was clear, logical, and comprehensible—resembled the verbal outrages of the imaginary Peasie Weasie, that "bold, bad man." Peasie Weasie's rocking, lilting puns and double entendres lurk somewhere in the depths of Groucho's repartee. This is from the famous contract routine in *A Night at the Opera:*

> FIORELLO (Chico): Ah, there's income tax . . .
>
> DRIFTWOOD (Groucho): Yes, there's a federal tax, and a state tax, and a city tax, and a street tax, and a sewer tax.
>
> FIORELLO: How much does this come to?
>
> DRIFTWOOD: Well, I figure if he doesn't sing too often, he can break even.
>
> FIORELLO: All right, we take it.
>
> DRIFTWOOD: All right, fine. Now here are the contracts. You just put his name at the top and you sign at the bottom. There's no need of you reading that because these are duplicates.
>
> FIORELLO: Yeah, they's a duplicates.
>
> DRIFTWOOD: I say they're duplicates.
>
> FIORELLO: Why sure they's a duplicates . . .
>
> DRIFTWOOD: Don't you know what duplicates are?
>
> FIORELLO: Sure. There's five kids up in Canada.
>
> DRIFTWOOD: Well, I wouldn't know about that. I haven't been to Canada in years. Well go ahead and read it.

The dialogue is barely removed from the primordial Peasie-Weasie inversions and contortions.

Like vaudeville's doggerel patter, Groucho's rapid-fire dialogue and Chico's off-kilter puns and manglings were created in the belly of the American metropolis in the years when the

American city was growing and becoming modern. The Brothers' language was an urban creation. Growing out of the modern city's money culture, it was as coarse and materialistic as the official or respectable language it took aim at.

The lament that the family did not have enough money reverberated around the young Julius. One reason that Minnie pushed her boys into show business was to make money, and the Brothers' goal in going on the road was to bring sufficient funds home. This, predictably, had a complicated effect on their attitude toward money. On the one hand, they disdained it. Chico gambled it away; Harpo became determined to live as easy a life as possible, money be damned; despite a growing love for show business, Groucho resented having to leave school to help support the family. At the same time, also predictably, the Brothers regarded money as the yardstick for happiness and success.

On top of all this, money in their comic art became, like sex, their most powerful means of undercutting any pretension to noble character and lofty sentiments. Contrary to the distaste experienced by Brooks Atkinson, there was nothing vulgar about that. Having seen from a young age how central money was to human endeavor, and how irrationally money's blessings were distributed among human beings, the Brothers undertook to push the reality of money into the face of the world, which pretended that money did not matter. What provoked them was the vulgarity of money being the ultimate arbiter of values and personal destiny. To the extent that their response itself was vulgar, per Atkinson, it was both a parody of money culture, and a taste administered to society of its own medicine.

It fell to Groucho, as the most intellectual and verbal of the Brothers, to illuminate the influence of money on human consciousness. In the first few moments of *Animal Crackers,* as Captain Spaulding is being celebrated by the elite rich for his nobility and bravery, he is haggling with the bearers of his sedan chair over the price of the ride. The routine's target is a transactional mentality that hides behind lofty notions of beauty and moral worth, and so the routine is conducted in transactional terms. Even Spaulding's remark after Mrs. Rittenhouse declares that the necklace that has just been stolen from her is worth $100,000—a vast sum of money at the time—comes across as a dissatisfaction with the current rate of exchange: "But is it valuable?" he asks, which implies that there are things in this life worth more than a mere fortune, yet also assumes that even those ethereal things have a price. They are not inestimable. They are "valuable." The transactional humor suggests an almost unbearable truth about human existence. Life is material, consisting of trades, trade-ins, and trade-offs. It is, in the world of the movie, both a truth that is abhorrent and a truth that must be lived by.

The doggerel patter of "Peasie Weasie" is where this coarse, hard, bullying, selfish, yet quasi-satirical hostility has its origins. Music, plus words, plus a context that replaces conventional meaning with new meaning equals a higher rationality, a more rigorously intellectual approach to social reality. It is also a higher type of conversion, or transaction. In their films, the Brothers brought Peasie Weasie out of vaudeville shtick into a social context. They monetized the English language.

The Peasie-Weasie style is alive and well today in rap, which also uses money culture to expose and deplore money's influence, even as it defiantly succumbs to it. Groucho would no doubt have been scandalized by the low-down grit of the language, though the misogyny might have struck a chord. But it was his style, forged in the crucible of the city, of being boldly solipsistic in the midst of sneakily selfish society that helped bring our contemporary Peasie Weasie to life.

5

Beyond the Pleasure Principle

ASSORTED VOICES: Doctor! Doctor! I don't know. Get away from me! No, we're not mad, just terribly hurt, that's all.
—*A Day at the Races*

IRVING THALBERG, dubbed the "Boy Wonder" of Hollywood, intuitively grasped the connection between the Marx Brothers' lives and their screen personas. Paramount had produced the films that made the Brothers famous: *The Cocoanuts, Animal Crackers, Monkey Business, Horse Feathers, Duck Soup*. But the flat box-office performance of *Duck Soup*, and its lukewarm critical reception, increased tensions the Brothers already had with the studio, and they left Paramount for good. So Chico, not unlike the shifty, fast-talking "business managers" he usually played onscreen, seized the social opportunity when he met Thalberg playing bridge and proceeded to charm the powerful studio executive. Thalberg didn't need much charming. He quickly persuaded Louis B. Mayer to bring the Marx Brothers on. In 1934, they signed a three-picture deal with MGM.

Much has been made of Thalberg's insight into the trajectory of the Marx Brothers' careers up to that point. But he had a keen understanding of their social and cultural context as well. He understood why the Marx Brothers' first five films appealed to Americans at the height of the Great Depression. Audiences were warmly receptive to a comic ensemble that, at a time of rapid transition from vaudeville to silent film to talkies, comprised an original synthesis of all three styles. Chico presented the stock figure of the immigrant, Harpo's pantomime was a reassuring echo of silent films, Groucho's insolent patter focused the talkies audience's attention on the spoken language as never before.

Yet the Brothers' excesses also parodied all three forms of entertainment. Chico's wily mangling of the English language made the immigrant seem more like your average self-interested American. Harpo's outrageous physical comedy seemed to mock silent films' solemn, outsized gestures. Groucho's use of "talk" served mainly to discredit talking as a reliable form of communication. The simultaneous affirmation and subversion of older forms of popular art reassured audiences living in a time of collapsing social realities.

Moviegoers in the late 1920s and early 1930s didn't seem to mind the fact that the typical plot of a Marx Brothers film was either thin or nonexistent. The grand American narrative of optimism and progress seemed to have suddenly dissolved. What the Marx Brothers offered, in a time of painful transformations, was the invincibility of character.

This was reflected in the best-selling novels of the time, whose protagonists were, for the most part, stronger than their plots. Some best-selling novels in 1931, the year that *Monkey*

Business was released, were *The Good Earth* by Pearl S. Buck, which featured a vividly drawn hero named Wang Lung, and *Shadows on the Rock* by Willa Cather, about the travails of two French colonists in Quebec in the seventeenth and eighteenth centuries. *Years of Grace* by Margaret Ayer Barnes, which won the Pulitzer Prize for that year, followed a woman named Jane Ward Carver from her teens to her fifties, the social landscape changing almost as rapidly as the scenes in a Marx Brothers film. Other novels with strong central characters were *The Road Back*, *The Bridge of Desire*, and *Back Street*, *road*, *bridge*, and *street* being words that captured a time of change and of yearning for stability.

By 1935, though, the New Deal had eased the effects of the Depression and the country was emerging into a new phase of relative prosperity. Thalberg understood that audiences now had little tolerance for plotless spectacles of mayhem. Lives had fallen back into place with all their illusions of following a comfortable narrative; America had a new national story to tell itself. Moviegoers wanted this new harmony to be reflected in new stories and new plots. With *A Night at the Opera* in 1935, and *A Day at the Races* two years later, Thalberg made night and day whole again, filling them up with romance and comedy.

The romance was important. The uninspiring box-office receipts for *Duck Soup* served to strengthen the sense that the Marx Brothers were leaving women members of the audience cold. Thalberg insisted that the movies they made for him have strong boy-girl subplots that women could identify with. In order to strengthen the serious dimension of the movies, he instructed a writer to come in and make an outline of the story without any gags. After that, he brought in comedy writers to supply the laughs.

Shrewdly, he hired writers who not only had worked well with the Marx Brothers before but were emotionally close to them. Despite *Duck Soup*'s commercial and critical failure,

Thalberg immediately acceded to Groucho's request that he bring on the two men responsible for that film's screenplay, Harry Ruby and Bert Kalmar. Both were longtime friends of the Brothers. Thalberg didn't like what they turned into him, though, and rejected their script. He hired two more writers, men who were not personally close to the Marx Brothers. Groucho gave them the thumbs down. Thalberg asked him what writers should be hired next. Groucho said he wanted George S. Kaufman, who had written the stage version of *The Cocoanuts*, and Morrie Ryskind, who had written the screenplays for *The Cocoanuts* and *Animal Crackers*. Both men had become intimates of Groucho and his brothers. Again, Thalberg immediately gave his assent.

Kaufman and Ryskind, rather than muting or modifying the personas the brothers had developed—a criticism often voiced by Marxian scholars—strengthened them by embedding them more naturally in the social context. They understood how the personas had grown organically from their actual personalities. So did Thalberg, who had the Brothers perform *A Night at the Opera* and *A Day at the Races* on stage throughout the country before making each film. Along with getting the audience's response to various gags and shticks so that he could see which to keep and which to drop, Thalberg knew that on stage the Brothers' fusion of their real selves and their stage personas was a natural process.

That stubborn synthesis of fragmented real self and unified fictional self was one primary element of the Brothers' appeal. They combined the immutable character of ideal romantic heroes with assaults upon the very notion of romantic heroes. They remained themselves, even as they were living proof of the unreliability, undignity, and unworthiness of their outrageously inadequate selves.

Groucho's glasses, bushy eyebrows, greasepaint mustache, and cigar may have grown out of vaudeville's stock figure of the so-called Dutch uncle, an unremittingly captious figure —shades of Minnie—who is constantly correcting, upbraiding, and scolding, but the disguise soon divulged his true identity. The glasses bespoke a cerebral figure; the mobile eyebrows insinuated that behind the glasses was a man who took nothing seriously; the greasepaint mustache proved that all appearances, social and personal, are either suspect or arbitrary or both. Words and images echo each other constantly in the work of the Marx Brothers, and this exchange between Captain Spaulding and Mrs. Rittenhouse from *Animal Crackers* illustrates one of Groucho's central visual principles:

> MRS. RITTENHOUSE: Captain Spaulding, you stand before me as one of the bravest men of all times.
>
> SPAULDING: Alright, I'll do that.

Standing the word *stand* on its head serves the same purpose as the elements of Groucho's appearance, each one of which qualifies or undercuts the other.

Groucho's walk, tested and perfected and a little bit different in every movie, has the same discombobulating effect. Groucho's gait is part strut and part slipping through and away from all those who walk and stand upright. It is no accident that four of the Brothers' first five films have names of animals in their titles, with *The Cocoanuts* virtually implying a simian presence. The wild-child, wild-animal element of their upbringing was a permanent feature of the brothers' adulthood, a quality that seemed to give them a special insight into the disjunction between language and behavior. You might say that even when Groucho is speaking, he is all behavior.

In *A Night at the Opera*, Kaufman and Ryskind drew on what they knew about the Marxes, and incorporated the collaborations and improvisations of the Brothers, especially Groucho, to add nuance and depth to their already established characters.

Take a look at Harpo's entrance in the film. When we first

see Harpo, he is wearing a clown suit and standing in a dressing room backstage at the Metropolitan Opera. Spraying water into his mouth, he tries to sing, but nothing comes out. He sprays the water into his mouth and attempts to sing several times, but—naturally—not a sound is heard.

Suddenly the door to the dressing room opens and in comes Rodolfo Lassparri, who we later learn is one of the greatest tenors in the world. We discover that Harpo's character, Tomasso, is Lassparri's dresser. When Lassparri catches Tomasso standing before his dressing room mirror in Lassparri's costume for *I Pagliacci*, Lassparri hits him in the back with his cane. But this isn't the usual madcap movie violence. Lassparri strikes Tomasso with unfunny force, and Harpo grimaces. Lassparri hits him again, in the same spot, with the same viciousness as before. The violence is so unfunny it is shocking.

Lassparri commands Tomasso to take off his clown suit. Tomasso obliges, but underneath the clown suit, he is wearing a naval uniform. He salutes Lassparri, who reacts with rage, shaking Tomasso and throwing him against the wall. "Take that off," he snarls. Tomasso divests himself of the sailor's uniform, only to next appear in a dress. He smiles at Lassparri. Lassparri chases Tomasso around the dressing room, threatening to break his neck.

Finally Harpo takes off the dress. Wearing a shirt and trousers, he continues to run away from Lassparri, at one point standing against the wall and wrapping himself in a curtain. Briefly he turns his eyes heavenward and smiles an angelic smile, one of his trademark facial expressions. Lassparri is, of course, not appeased. Rather, the show of innocence and vulnerability incites his sadism even more. He shouts that he is firing Tomasso, proceeding to lash him savagely with a bullwhip that he has pulled off a hook on the wall. He continues to whip Tomasso, who opens the door and, receiving one last wallop from

Lassparri, falls out of the dressing room onto the floor of the hallway outside. That is where Kitty Carlisle, one half of the movie's boy-girl love story, sees him. She looks at Tomasso with deadly seriousness and grave alarm. Her face sums up the import of the whole scene. Underneath Harpo's trademark hijinks there is nothing humorous going on here.

The same thing happens when we first see Harpo a few minutes into *A Day at the Races*, the second film the Marx Brothers made for Thalberg and MGM, two years after *A Night at the Opera* had been a smash hit at the box office. Though Kaufman and Ryskind had nothing to do with the movie, the small crowd of people who did collaborate on *A Day at the Races*' screenplay obviously built on the plot of the previous film.

One of the strongest echoes is Harpo's introductory scene. He plays a jockey named Stuffy and when we first encounter him, he is about to win a race. Returning to the stables, he runs into J. D. Morgan, a no-good banker who owns the horse Stuffy has just ridden to victory. Morgan kicks Stuffy in the behind. "I told you to lose that race," he says. Then he punches Stuffy in the face. Stuffy dashes out of the stable with Morgan in hot pursuit, and successfully eludes him. The scene is less violent than the one in the dressing room in *A Night at the Opera*, but it is violent, jarring, and unfunny nonetheless.

Here is Harpo's account, in his autobiography, of why he dropped out of school in second grade, at the age of eight:

> My formal schooling ended halfway through my second crack at the second grade, at which time I left school the most direct way possible. I was thrown out the window.
>
> There were two causes of this. One was a big Irish kid in my class and the other was a bigger Irish kid. I was a perfect patsy for them, a marked victim. I was small for my age. I had a high, squeaky voice. And I was the only Jewish boy in the room. . . .

> Every once in a while, when Miss Flatto [the teacher] left the room, the Irishers would pick me up and throw me out the window, into the street. Fortunately our room was on the first floor. The drop was about eight feet—high enough for a good jolt but low enough not to break any bones.
>
> I would pick myself up, dust myself off, and return to the classroom as soon as I was sure the teacher was back. I would explain to Miss Flatto that I had been to the toilet. I knew that if I squealed I'd get worse than a heave out the window. . . . She began sending notes to my mother, all with the same warning:
>
> Something had better be done about straightening me out or I would be a disgrace to my family, my community, and my country.

Harpo then shifts into a bit of dubiously truthful vaudeville. He tells of his mother sending his cousin Polly's boyfriend, a fishmonger, to the classroom to consult with Miss Flatto, the boyfriend coming into the class "fish buckets and all." The smell of fish, Harpo says, sickened Miss Flatto, who kicked the emissary out of school. This incited Harpo's persecutors even further. "The two Irish boys now gave me the heave-ho every chance they got, which was three or four times a day. . . . So one sunny day when Miss Flatto left the room and I was promptly heaved into the street, I picked myself up, turned my back on P.S. 86 and walked straight home, and that was the end of my formal education."

The "tears of a clown" are proverbial, the phrase meant to convey the hurt at the core of people who earn their living making audiences laugh—Harpo's wearing the clown's costume at the beginning of *A Night at the Opera* gestures explicitly to this platitude. The hackneyed idea is that a creative comical will transfigures the wound into humor. The Marx Brothers offer a different comedic model. They channeled the wound directly into the humor without any kind of transfiguration at all. The pain is not repressed, suppressed, sublimated, or converted. It is a transparent and crucial component of the joke, whether it is the neglected Julius speaking ever more outrageously in order to be heard, or Harpo turning the trauma of being brutalized as a child into the inability to speak. Or putting the villain into the clown suit, as well as the victim.

It is fair to assume that Kaufman and Ryskind, being intimates of the Marxes, were familiar with Harpo's brutalization at the hands of the two Irish bullies. Even if they weren't, they were so open to the Marx Brothers' interventions in the script that they would easily have incorporated into the film most anything the brothers asked for. As Wes Gehring has written, both Harpo and Groucho were ultimately responsible for their own material. The savage beating of Harpo at the beginning of each movie is like one of those prequels that explain the genesis of Superman or Batman. The audience is being visually instructed in Harpo's beginnings. His muteness is the springboard of many a gag and laugh. But his muteness is at its core an inability to speak, and the inability to speak is the product of trauma.

It hardly seems a coincidence that this bit of autobiography makes its appearance most explicitly in the first two films the brothers did for Paramount. Thalberg's desire that the brothers henceforth make more of an appeal to women in the audience was reflected in the pained and compassionate expression on Kitty Carlisle's face when she sees the beaten and humiliated Tomasso tumble out of Lassparri's dressing room into the hallway. In that one instant, Harpo was transformed from a plague on women's sanity and safety, as he chases them around in one place or another, to an object of their compassion.

Thalberg brought out a strain that had always been present in Harpo because Harpo himself had carried it with him, as it were, into his art. There had always been a pathos to Harpo's muteness. The more aggressive it made him, and the more furiously he chased screaming women around while honking his horn, the more desperate and thus vulnerable his outrages proved him to be. The Marx Brothers' first six films, done for Paramount, stress the bright side of Harpo's vulnerability. He is never savagely beaten, and is manhandled only by Chico, who is also his co-conspirator. His Gookie faces, and angelic faces, and generally otherworldly faces find their affinity in children, who are the only people in those films who fully accept Harpo, and who seem to have some mysterious understanding of who he really is.

The jolting moment in these films, for all their plotless chaos, is when Harpo sits down to play the harp. He could not be more unlike Chico, whose piano-playing antics—"shooting" the keys, turning musical notes into jokes and punchlines, destroying the piano itself just as he destroys the English language—reflected his sneaky, subversive persona and personality. Harpo at the harp is worlds away from Harpo the outrageous mime. The minute he sits down at the harp, his features relax into a natural expression. He grows serious. He suddenly has something that no one else has in the cinematic worlds the Marx Brothers create: a vocation.

The characters Groucho plays, from Mr. Hammer the hotel owner, to Captain Spaulding the explorer, to Professor Wagstaff and beyond, are all frauds pretending to be someone with a more or less conventional position in life—a weird refraction of the fact that Julius was pretending to be Groucho, who was more real than Julius would ever be. Chico was a con man with a vapid center, even when he played the piano. But Harpo at the harp brings to mind Auden's lines:

> You need not see what someone is doing
> to know if it is his vocation

you have only to watch his eyes:
a cook mixing a sauce, a surgeon

making a primary incision,
a clerk completing a bill of lading,

wear the same rapt expression,
forgetting themselves in a function.

How beautiful it is,
that eye-on-the-object look.

Or as Harpo writes in his autobiography about the difference between himself and his character: "When he's chasing a girl across the screen, it's Him. When he sits down to play the harp, it's Me. Whenever I touch the strings of the harp, I stopped being an actor."

He didn't realize—how could he have?—to what extent that division he saw in himself reflected his actual life. That is the personal tragedy Thalberg brought to the surface. Harpo bullies as he was bullied, he puts his leg into another person's hand and thus into another person's power, he chases the helpless and gets chased by those who can hurt him. Then he finds his vocation. He loses himself in the waking dream of performing on his harp—a perfect state of play, which is a childlike raptness. No wonder children look on him as being just like them.

In that moment when Harpo sits down to play the harp, you see both his spiritual destiny fulfilled and the sadness of his never being able to find himself in society. The irony of his harp playing is that the harp gives him his voice, but the harp is too otherworldly to make social sense.

To be understood, all of Harpo's elements have to be grasped in one intuitive leap. He is like a poem. That is why, though Groucho was the intellectual of the trio, the one with the clever verbal patter and the multifarious antisocial gestures, Harpo was the one brother who appealed to the literati.

Alexander Woollcott, the *New Yorker*'s mordant and influential theater critic, fell in love with Harpo. He pursued the helpless-seeming clown's friendship from the time he saw the Brothers in their 1924 Broadway debut, *I'll Say She Is!*, and inducted Harpo as a regular at the famed Algonquin Round Table, with other wits such as Dorothy Parker and Robert Benchley. Harpo warmly returned Woollcott's friendship, but it was a different story with Groucho. A dinner between the two men was typical of their relationship. When the waiter brought Groucho his food first, making Woollcott wait for his, the critic fumed. At one point, the waiter returned to the table and asked, "What was it that Mr. Woollcott ordered?" "Muffins," snapped Woollcott. "Filled with pus." Groucho stood up and stormed out of the Algonquin.

It's easy to see why the Algonquin wits, who complained that Groucho was "suspicious and hostile," "arrogant and superior," had trouble tolerating him. The Ariel-like Harpo was pure id, sidling up adoringly to any source of pleasure, fleeing with distaste from the slightest postponement of gratification. Groucho, for all his chaotic subversions of language and propriety and convention onscreen, was the sternest of the brothers, the most dissatisfied. He was the superego of the Marx Brothers. He had all the hypercritical, unhappy discontent of the intellectual. The Algonquin wits, who felt themselves both superior and inferior to intellectuals, disdained and feared him.

Beside Harpo, Groucho strikes a powerful contrast. Groucho, though he has the reputation of being the very apotheosis of the Marx Brothers' style of "lunatic comedy," as it has inaccurately been called, is, alongside Harpo's hybrid of comic meanness and ethereal poignancy, like the austere father representing the reality principle. It might be hard to think of *A Night at the Opera*'s Otis B. Driftwood or *A Day at the Races*' Dr. Hugo Z. Hackenbush as embodying the reality principle, but the sudden appearance of Groucho calms the riot of thoughts and feelings Harpo's poetically layered character provokes.

In *A Night at the Opera,* Lassparri, after he has beaten Tomasso, attacks him again after Kitty Carlisle rejects his romantic overtures to her. Suddenly Driftwood appears and speaks his immortal lines, "Hey, you big bully. What's the idea of hitting that little bully?" Lassparri, wearing a clown costume, pushes Tomasso away with one last vicious slap in the face and turns belligerently to Driftwood. "Now whaddya got to say to me?" he says to Driftwood with an air of menace. "Just this," replies Driftwood. "Can you sleep on your stomach with such big buttons on your pajamas?" Then he pulls one of the buttons off Lassparri's costume. "Why, you," snarls Lassparri. He pulls his hand back, about to strike Driftwood, but Tomasso comes up from behind and hits him over the head with a mallet, knocking him unconscious.

Driftwood flinches slightly, then follows Tomasso as he pulls the unconscious Lassparri off to the side. "Nice work, I think you got him," says Driftwood. Tomasso takes some smelling salts out of his pocket and waves them under Lassparri's nose. "Ah, smelling salts," says Driftwood. "That'll bring him to." Tomasso continues administering the salts. "You're sorry for what you did, eh?" says Driftwood. Tomasso turns to him and nods solemnly. "That shows a nice spirit," Driftwood says. Tomasso continues with the smelling salts and Lassparri slowly starts to sit up. "Now he's coming along," Driftwood says, the cigar back in his mouth. "He'll be fine now." Tomasso makes a mad little smile and with impish intensity hits Lassparri over the head with the mallet again, knocking him unconscious a second time. The demonic expression on his face is like the obverse side of the "beautiful . . . eye-on-the-object look" he has when he sits down to play the harp.

Wild-eyed with sudden panic, Harpo runs off, but not before making the surpassingly strange gesture of placing his finger on Driftwood's shadow, which is on the wall next to him, and then running his finger along part of the shadow before disappearing. Driftwood puts his foot on Lassparri's motionless body and takes the cigar out of his mouth. "Get fresh with me, eh?" he says, flicking an ash onto Lassparri. Chico enters.

In a few masterful strokes, the comedy is pulled back from the poetic-rambunctious precipice Harpo has brought it to and restored to a social context. The violence of Harpo's mallet gives way to Groucho's insolent quip about the buttons. Groucho himself might be the destabilizing element in any social situation, but here he reimposes order. That is why Lassparri cannot hit him. No one ever hits Groucho's characters. They are protected by their function, which is to bring Harpo's chaos to a close. That is another reason the Brothers remain timeless. Each one is a complete, self-created world that follows its own unique law.

The Brothers intersect with one another, but they cannot be said to actually interact. They run parallel to each other even when they have the appearance of interacting. Groucho's remark "That shows a nice spirit" is immediately followed by Harpo's lapse back into the role of little bully, smacking Lassparri over the head with Lassparri's own viciousness. Groucho placing his foot on Lassparri and flicking his ash swings the pendulum back to a comedy of manners—bad manners, no doubt, but still manners. What we see is drawing room comedy and opera buffa simultaneously. It is similar to when small children engage in "parallel play."

Groucho's off-the-cuff remark "That shows a nice spirit" serves a practical purpose. It immediately moves Harpo's comic violence into the social realm. "That shows a nice spirit" is funny coming after the whack Harpo has given Lassparri on the head. Shifting the movie's gears into verbal mode, it is an apt prelude to the following scene, which consists of the famous contract routine: "There ain't no Sanity Clause!" There Groucho negotiates a deal with Chico in order to retain "the greatest tenor in the world," unwittingly retaining from the shifty Chico an unproven talent named Ricardo Baroni. The scene with Harpo and Lassparri was living proof of the world's lack of a sanity clause.

When Harpo hit Lassparri again, Groucho had to make the transition even more vigorous, so he himself employed physical comedy, but with an intellectual slant that appeals to the mind, not just the senses. Putting his foot on Lassparri and flicking his cigar ashes onto Lassparri—a rude employment of a quintessentially civilized ritual—Groucho both reiterates Harpo's slapstick and eases the audience out of it. "Get fresh with me, eh?" brings you sharply into Groucho's social, verbal world. It is something a woman would say—it is Groucho's trademark to regularly, with the slightest touch, impersonate the women who bedeviled him when a child in the same way that Harpo impersonated the bullies who tormented him.

We go from an instruction in the nature of Harpo, a bully traumatized by bullies, and a masochist reenacting his trauma, to a lesson in Groucho—the young boy wounded by his mother, then afflicted by a woman during his first sexual encounter, who becomes the comic actor both deriding women's vulnerability and using his impersonation of a woman to disclose his own.

Never before in American comedy had the real personalities of comic actors blurred into their stage personas so completely. One of the results was that the comedy often played second banana to the nihilism of a self-expression that fed off social situations, but that was completely detached from them. When Harpo mysteriously touches Groucho's shadow, he is pointing to the Brothers' essential nature as performers. Just as light creates a shadow whose reality is an illusion, so society makes the Brothers' performances possible, despite that fact that they are like ghosts in the midst of real people.

This is not to say that Harpo's look of fright after he runs his finger along Groucho's shadow cannot have a more specific meaning. By 1935, the year *A Night at the Opera* was released, Italy had become a full-blown fascist state. In its opening moments the film originally included references that made it clear Italy was where the action begins. Groucho asks Chico whether he's Italian, and Chico replies that only his mother and father are. Then he pronounces his father's Italian name. Censors removed all that dialogue, apparently because the studio did not want Italy to be portrayed sympathetically at a time when the country had become a dictatorship. The original print has been lost, and though it is now less clear that the movie begins in Italy, there can be no doubt that it does. Groucho's first exchange with Chico hints at the gathering storm:

> DRIFTWOOD: Well, things seem to be getting better around the country.
>
> FIORELLO: I don't know. I'm a stranger here myself. [Itself a line that elicits an incredulous look from Groucho and is funny on two levels: Chico's Italian accent makes him seem like a native, not a stranger; Chico's phony Italian accent proves that he really is a stranger.]

Whatever Harpo meant by running his finger over Groucho's shadow, his eerie gesture points to a familiarity with the shadow world, a world that the Brothers inhabited with inborn ease. The long exchange between Driftwood and Fiorello that follows also draws from the Brothers' actual personalities. The real-life Chico was a petty thief, former con man, wily business manager, and compulsive gambler. "I guess I have lost around two million dollars gambling," he confessed later in life. "I had money. I lost it. Las Vegas, the races, women." In

A Night at the Opera, Chico becomes the crafty Fiorello, who cheats Driftwood, who thinks he is cheating him.

The comedy flees deeper and deeper into a negative space. After Lassparri's vicious beating of Tomasso, you uncomfortably realize that the "greatest tenor in the world," whom Driftwood is trying to sign up, is, in fact, Lassparri himself.

6

Groucho the Jewish Aristocrat

Character is everything.
—Groucho Marx

"We Marx Brothers never denied our Jewishness," Groucho once said. "We simply didn't use it. We could have safely fallen back on the Yiddish theater, making secure careers for ourselves. But our act was designed from the start to have a broad appeal." For all that, Groucho, more than his brothers, is identified with the spirit of Jewish humor, so much so that the cover of a recent book called *No Joke: Making Jewish Humor*, by Ruth Wisse, sports an image consisting of Groucho's trademark bushy black eyebrows, large nose, and bushy mustache. This despite the fact that Wisse barely mentions Groucho at all, and describes him as "neutering Jewishness for a general public." Ouch.

Which raises the inevitable question of just what is Jewish humor. One recalls a famous remark by Bernard Malamud, who is considered the quintessential Jewish writer, though his themes of mercy and redemption are Christian in nature. "All men are Jews," he once said. "Though few men know it." Malamud meant that the Jewish travail of displacement, wandering, and persecution is in fact a universal experience, the lot of humankind. In that perspective, the "broad appeal" Groucho spoke of—Chico's guile, Harpo's outraged innocence, Groucho's corrosive nihilism—is really a Jewish frame of reference, born perhaps in the displacements of immigration, that speaks to all people.

But Malamud's notion of the universality of Jewish experience is itself a Jewish idea. And Groucho's idiom, as devoid of specific Jewish references as it may be, nevertheless came out of his own experience, which was, culturally at least, Jewish to the core.

Groucho's famous quip about not wanting to belong to any club that would have him as a member is the one line of his that has lasted through posterity. It is the only example of Groucho's verbal wit that Wisse includes in her book. She writes: " 'I don't want to join any club that would have me as a member,' said Groucho Marx, lampooning the Jew in himself who disdains the welcome of his own kind in favor of the restrictions placed on him by others." Professor Wisse, the Martin Peretz Professor of Yiddish literature and comparative literature at Harvard University, concludes: "Since the presumptive appeal of Groucho's joke is proportional to one's discomfort with one's identity, it bears noting that this became his most famous line."

Wisse's interpretation of the line reflects how it has always been understood. Perhaps the most famous expression of that perspective occurs in *Annie Hall*, written and directed by Woody Allen, a younger comic whom Groucho greatly admired. At the beginning of the movie, Alvy Singer, played by Allen, looks at the camera and delivers a short monologue:

> The—the other important joke for me is one that's, uh, usually attributed to Groucho Marx but I think it appears originally in Freud's *Wit and Its Relation to the Unconscious.* And it goes like this—I'm paraphrasing: Uh . . . "I would never wanna belong to any club that would have someone like me for a member." That's the key joke of my adult life in terms of my relationships with women.

Later, Alvy proves his point when he finds himself stopping in the midst of sexual intercourse with Allison Portchnik to discuss John F. Kennedy's assassination. She says to him: "You're using this conspiracy theory as an excuse to avoid sex with me." Alvy then addresses another monologue to the audience:

> Oh, my God! (*To the camera*) She's right! Why did I turn off Allison Portchnik? She was—she was beautiful. She was willing. She was real . . . intelligent. (*Sighing*) Is it the old Groucho Marx joke? That—that I—I just don't wanna belong to any club that would have someone like me for a member?

Like Wisse, Allen understands Groucho's remark to be the epitome of self-loathing. And since Allen himself is the epitome of Jewish humor, the most gifted and versatile apostle of the seemingly self-loathing vein in Jewish comedy, his use of Groucho's quip firmly established it as the ur-Jewish joke, and established self-hatred as the essence of Jewish humor.

Wisse herself, after deftly exploring just about every different phase and style of Jewish humor, ends her book on a reductive note. After observing that the great Jewish comic artists and wits of modern Germany—Heine, Max Liebermann, Ernst Lubitsch, Kurt Tucholsky—"ended in exile and some in suicide, their works banned and burned by the masters of German politics," she writes that "getting a joke may indeed be the last cultural bond among Jews headed for doom—or doomed to be Jews." She goes on to reach the depressingly familiar conclusion that what characterizes Jewish humor, unlike other types of humor, is "moral self-correction and self-accountability," qualities that amount to a self-hatred that ends in exile and suicide, and worse.

Though, as I wrote, Wisse ranges widely throughout Jewish history, she derives her conclusions from the humor prevalent in the shtetls of the nineteenth and early twentieth centuries, and among immigrant Jews in America in the early part of the twentieth. This makes it hard to determine what is Jewish in the humor, and what is the result of economic suffering and social prejudice, cultural displacement, and social marginalization.

Yet even Yiddish humor, famous for its dark self-deprecating irony, and the modern American Jewish humor that evolved from it, are a lot more complicated than an exercise in self-lacerating "moral self-correction and self-accountability." Allow me to demonstrate that point with an incident involving the very Martin Peretz who endowed Professor Wisse's chair.

I once worked at the *New Republic* magazine, which at the time was owned by Peretz. I was hired by the magazine's literary editor, Leon Wieseltier, but I had to meet with Peretz before I could be brought on board. One beautiful spring day in early June, Peretz summoned me to breakfast at the Regency Hotel in Manhattan, where some of the city's Jewish elite liked to take their morning meal.

Peretz was in a line of illustrious descendants. One of his ancestors was the famous Yiddish writer I. L. Peretz. The elder Peretz's most famous and beloved story was called "Bontsha the Silent," about a man so poor that when he dies, the angels make a grand gesture. The head angel tells him that all of Paradise is his. "Whatever you want!" he says. "Everything is yours!" But Bontsha has been so reduced by life that he lowers his eyes and replies softly, "What I would like is to have, every morning for breakfast, a hot roll with fresh butter." The angels hang their heads, ashamed at having created a human being so meek and abject.

That morning at the Regency, Peretz smiled at me and gestured to the thick, oversized menu I was holding in my hands. "You can have anything you want," he said warmly. "Whatever you want." I could hardly resist. "What I would like," I said, "is to have a hot roll with fresh butter." Peretz looked at me in astonishment, and then roared with laughter. When I got home, a message from Wieseltier was on my answering machine. "The Bontsha gambit worked," he said. "You're hired." The sentimental Jewish story was the perfect occasion for a serendipitous Jewish joke.

Yiddish literature walks a fine line between sentiment and sentimentality. In doing so, it walks a fine line between drama and comedy. It is so suffused with feeling that the application of an intellectual touch often transforms a poignant sentiment into a humorous one. "Bontsha the Silent" turns on a sudden ironic reversal at the end. Sudden ironic reversals are also often the stuff of Jewish humor.

For example. A husband and wife are walking along the promenade in Odessa. A beautiful young woman walks by. "Who is that?" asks the wife. "That is Goldberg's mistress," replies the husband. "Ah," says the wife. They keep walking. Another beautiful young woman walks by. "Who is that?" asks the wife. "That is Cohen's mistress," replies the husband. "Ah," says the wife. They continue walking. Another beautiful young woman walks by. "And who is that?" asks the wife. "That is my mistress," replies the husband. "Ohhh," says the wife. "Ours is the best." The reversal is the wife's pride over, rather than anger at, her husband's infidelity. The irony is that she is so obsessed with social status that she cannot see her own humiliation.

The reversal in "Bontsha" is that the humble man, instead of doing the predictable thing, and asking for something that would gratify his senses beyond his wildest mortal dreams, asks only for that spare, simple meal. The irony is that what appears a humble request in heaven was, for him, an exorbitant luxury in life. The formal structure of the heartrending story is identical to that of the—to my mind, anyway—hilarious joke. That is why it so easily lent itself to the humorous treatment I gave it at the breakfast with Peretz. I applied an intellectual twist, a self-interested irony on top of its sentimental irony, and presto! A sad story became the catalyst for a humorous incident.

Is "Bontsha" the product of a culture where such meekness and abjection are common? Is the joke from Odessa the product of a culture where crass materiality blinds people to their own mortification?

One of the problems with so many interpretations of the meaning of jokes is that the interpreter looks solely at the content of the joke, rather than the moral position of the person who is telling the joke. The man who wrote "Bontsha" has a potent creative will that his character completely lacks. It is so powerful that the author audaciously inhabits the psychology of angels. If you stick with the content of the joke, you might be able to conclude that abject humility was the dominant trait of eastern European Jews in the late nineteenth century, which was around the time I. L. Peretz wrote his story. If you look at the man who wrote it, you get a different impression of his milieu. Peretz was a lawyer with a prosperous practice who became a powerful official in Warsaw's Jewish community. Clearly he expected his readers to grasp the import of "Bontsha" from a critical distance. If they had all been Bontshas, they would not have understood the fullness of the story.

In the same way, a cultural historian could use the joke from Odessa to demonstrate the crude lack of spirituality and self-awareness that was prevalent in the Russian-Jewish community. But that would ignore the total context surrounding the joke. It was told by someone to other people; perhaps it was first told by a comedian to an audience. The man, or woman, who told it found it funny precisely because he or she was superior to the wife in the joke. The people who heard the joke laughed because they occupied the same moral position as the teller. What the joke could well prove—if it proves anything general about Jewish culture—is that the moral obtuseness of the wife in the joke was as rare in the Jewish life of that time and place as it was recognizable.

This puts the classic joke about Jewish meekness and passivity in a different perspective. Two Jews are standing blindfolded against a wall facing a firing squad. One Jew turns to the other. "I'm going to ask for a cigarette," he says. "No, no!" whispers the other Jew. "Don't make trouble!" Where does the accurate representation of Jewish experience lie, in the content of the joke, which portrays Jews as absurdly timid and frightened, or with the inventor or the teller of the joke, as well as with the people who relish it—all of whom are savvy and ironic enough to mock a certain Jewish tendency toward passivity, which may have been either a dominant Jewish trait of the time or a minor tendency that irritated sensitive Jewish consciences?

The question of what is the essential quality of Jewish humor is no small thing. In *Eichmann in Jerusalem*, Hannah Arendt portrayed eastern European Jews as going passively to the gas chambers like sheep. Subsequent books presented a contrary picture, depicting Jews as ambushed by an unprecedented historical situation that overtook them slowly, one seemingly innocuous detail at a time. These books emphasize Jewish attempts at escape, resistance, and revenge.

The Jewish humor of the shtetls that has come down to us through countless Jewish comedians and wits since the great waves of Jewish immigration at the end of the nineteenth century and the beginning of the twentieth is what has defined our sense of the character of Jewish humor. This makes the identification of Jewish humor with self-loathing problematic. It reduces Jewish humor to a relatively narrow historical experience in the six thousand–year history of the Jewish people. Thomas Mann cherished a story told by Max Brod, Kafka's closest friend, about Kafka reading *The Trial* out loud to a group of intimates in Prague, who laughed "immoderately," as Brod recalled, during the entire first chapter. The novel, a parable of masochism and guilt, must have struck a chord in these Jewish sons. But it is doubtful that anyone would find that novel's chilling opening pages funny today.

Indeed, as a result of expanded opportunities and a lessening of religious prejudice in American, a note of withering disdain appeared in Jewish humor and wit, a moral superiority to that high Western culture from which Jews had been excluded for so long. Sometime in the mid-twentieth century, the American-Jewish poet Delmore Schwartz opened an essay that he called "Existentialism: The Inside Story" like this: "*Existentialism means that no one else can take a bath for you.* This example is suggested by Heidegger, who points out that no one else can die for you. But the same is true of taking a bath." There are resonances here with Professor Wagstaff's biology lecture, not to mention echoes of Captain Spaulding's very un-self-loathingly parody of Eugene O'Neill's portentous language in *Strange Interlude:*

> Pardon me while I have a strange interlude. Why, you couple of baboons! What makes you think I'd marry either one of you! Strange how the wind blows tonight. It has a thin, eerie voice, reminds me of poor old Moslin. How happy I could be with either of these two if both of them just went away!

Here is the exemplary comic of Jewish self-detestation patronizing the most celebrated American playwright of the time.

The equation of Jewish humor with self-loathing has another difficulty. It refuses to acknowledge that in so many Jewish jokes themselves the source and the effect of self-disparagement is confidence, power, and a sense of one's own moral superiority. Wisdom is a supreme form of self-possession and self-confidence, and the very shape of Jewish wisdom can possess the contours of a joke—just as Jewish jokes often possess the contours of Jewish wisdom tales. Two men meet on the street. One man says to the other, "How are you?" The other man says, "Not so good." "What's wrong?" asks the first man. "Well," says the second man, "I thought that I would sell some of my old clothes and buy some new ones." "What's wrong with that?" "I sold them at Silverman's store on Thursday. On Friday I went back to Silverman's and used the money to buy a whole new wardrobe. When I got home and opened the boxes, I saw that I had bought the clothes I sold the day before."

Hasidic saying: "If we could hang all our sorrows on pegs and were allowed to choose those we liked best, every one of us would take back his own, for all the rest would seem even more difficult to bear." Forgive my concoction of the meagerly funny—if funny at all—joke. I want to show how entwined Jewish humor is with Jewish wisdom, and that behind the self-deprecating style of Jewish humor is, not just the aggression that always lurks in wit, but a robust sense of one's own intelligence and worldliness. Groucho may not have liked Julius, but he adored Groucho.

In 2007, Richard Raskin, an American professor of esthetics and communication at Aarhus University in Denmark, posted on his website an essay about what he called Groucho's "Resignation Letter." So far as I know, it is the only serious analysis of Groucho's famous line ever written.

Raskin begins by clearing up a few matters. For one thing, he points out that Woody Allen was wrong to attribute Groucho's seemingly self-denigrating joke to Freud. Rather—as I pointed out in an earlier chapter—it appears in a different form in Theodor Reik's *Jewish Wit*. For another, Groucho's remark was not some off-the-cuff quip meant to entertain. It appeared in a specific social context. Raskin quotes from the memoir of Groucho written by son Arthur Marx:

> [The actor, Georgie] Jessel has always been able to make Father laugh, and as a favor to him, he joined the Hollywood chapter of the Friar's Club a couple of years ago. But Father doesn't like club life, and, after a few months, he dropped out. The Friars were disappointed over losing him, and wanted to know why he was resigning. They weren't satisfied with his original explanation—that he just didn't have time to participate in the club's activities. He must have another, more valid reason, they felt.
>
> "I do have another reason," he wrote back promptly. "I didn't want to tell you, but since you've forced the issue, I just don't want to belong to any club that would have me as a member."

Raskin then goes on to quote from a second source: Groucho's own autobiography, *Groucho and Me:*

> Some years ago, after considerable urging, I consented to join a prominent theatrical organization. By an odd coincidence, it was called the Delaney Club. Here, I thought, within these hallowed walls of Thespis, we would sit of an evening with our Napoleon brandies and long-stemmed pipes and discuss Chaucer, Charles Lamb, Ruskin, Voltaire, Booth, the Barrymores, Duse, Shakespeare, Bernhardt and all the other legendary figures of the theatre and literature. The first night I went there, I found thirty-two fellows playing gin rummy with marked cards . . . and four members in separate phone booths calling women who were other members' wives. A few nights later . . . I was sitting next to a barber who had cut me many times, both socially and with a

> razor. At one point he looked slowly around the room, then turned to me and said, "Groucho, we're certainly getting a lousy batch of new members!"
>
> I chose to ignore this remark and tried talking to him about Chaucer, Ruskin and Shakespeare, but he had switched to denouncing electric razors as a death blow to the tonsorial arts, so I dried up and resumed drinking. The following morning I sent the club a wire stating, PLEASE ACCEPT MY RESIGNATION. I DON'T WANT TO BELONG TO ANY CLUB THAT WILL ACCEPT ME AS A MEMBER.

Raskin concludes that "paradoxically, one of the most striking examples of a self-disparaging joke turns out to have been motivated by a wish on the jokester's part to dissociate himself once and for all from a group of people to whom he felt superior." We might add that this quality puts Groucho's line in the same category as the joke from Odessa and Bontsha the Silent. In all three cases, the supposed self-disparaging Jew is operating from behind examples of—or in Groucho's case, the appearance of—self-disparagement for the purpose of exercising intellectual and social power. "Never trust the teller," wrote D. H. Lawrence. "Trust the tale." The opposite is true in matters of comedy or wit. Never trust the joke. Trust the joker.

Raskin even performs the public service of demonstrating the universality of a self-disparaging wit. He quotes from a letter that Abraham Lincoln wrote to Eliza Browning in 1838. Lincoln writes, "I can never be satisfied with anyone who would be block head enough to have me." Self-disparagement, and all its many cousins, from British self-deprecation to today's "humble boast" is hardly a specifically Jewish trait. The idea that the essence of Jewish humor is self-dislike might not have caught on at all if it had not been for Freud, who in *Jokes and Their Relation to the Unconscious* stigmatized Jewish humor for all time as being derived from Jewish feelings of inadequacy. That book is as much a product of the young Freud witnessing his father's humiliation at the hands of antisemitic bullies on a Viennese street as wry Jewish irony is the creation of the shtetls.

Still, for all his astute analysis of Groucho's line, Raskin does not address a fundamental question: Why did Groucho choose to use a pretext of self-loathing to resign from the club at all? Surely there were other explanations he could have given in order to spare the feelings of the club members, if that was indeed his aim. The fact is that the episode is yet one more example of how Groucho used self-negation as a path to freedom and power.

Despite its obvious exaggeration and air of shtick, Groucho's account of his thinking at the time seems more than plausible. As usual, he is performing his actual life; he is enacting his subconscious. He begins with the fantasy of high culture that he harbored his entire life. At the club, his expectation is that he will be able to talk with the other members about all the literary greats. Instead he is back in the Yorkville apartment where he grew up, with everyone gambling and philandering.

He then finds himself sitting next to someone who, while probably not a barber, feels superior to Groucho. He insults Groucho by putting down the new group of inductees, of which Groucho is a member. This is too much for a man who, with his brothers, spent sixteen years on the harsh, wounding vaudeville circuit, treated as a second-class citizen, disdained and shunned in the small towns he played. Abruptly reminded that he is, for all his wealth and fame, a mere entertainer, Groucho inflates himself into a literary intellectual and dismisses the man—in this written account—by demonstrating that he is unable to talk with Groucho about literature. Then, according to his autobiography, he sits down and writes his famous telegram.

Feelings of exclusion marked Groucho's entire life. His and his brothers' sharp sense of themselves as outsiders was perhaps one reason that they felt truly comfortable only when they were with one another, and perhaps why they are so successful as a trio.

Having felt excluded for most of his life, Groucho can express his insult only in terms of inclusion versus exclusion. Never having been able to become a member of a club he once wanted passionately to join—normal society—he rejects the club that will have him, but only because that club reminds him of the origins it took him so long to escape. The interminable irony of the joke lies, as does all of Groucho's humor, in the exposure of his psyche.

If there is anything characteristically Jewish in Groucho's famous line it is in the way he uses his life to eclipse a social situation; in the way he negates the world around him to carve out a private freedom. From Heine, to Freud, to Larry David and Sacha Baron Cohen, Jewish humor has broken new ground in the realm of subjectivity. That is to say, by means of a psychological inwardness whose acuity and depth confer a rare distinction on the humbly born and the marginally situated, Jewish humor endowed social outsiders with a power they did not possess before; it has made the outsider a permanent fixture of mainstream American public life. The status of the outsider is one place to begin to construct a definition of Jewish humor.

7

Groucho the Jewish Outsider-Philosopher

People struggling for a living, starving and all kinds of riots. . . . No, I don't think the world is funny.
—Groucho Marx on William F. Buckley Jr.'s *Firing Line*, July 1967

THE COMIC'S role as outsider is a modern development. Though early Greek comic playwrights practiced a frank-speaking style, the characters who delivered satiric truths occupied clear social niches in the play's reflected social world. Satirists from Juvenal to Boccaccio to Swift, Pope, Byron, Bierce, and Twain dramatized social injustice, hypocrisy, the fathomless ambiguity of human nature, but they rarely, if ever, presented the spectacle, in their work itself, of insulting the pillars of society directly, let alone celebrated a fictional situation in which their characters created social conflict themselves.

Groucho, the product par excellence of Jewish displacement, was the first comic figure to explicitly appear in a social situation while clearly existing outside it. Chaplin's Little Tramp lives on society's margins. W. C. Fields's misanthropic persona was so exaggerated in his aversions to children and small animals that the audience found him irresistibly endearing. They instantly warmed to him in those movies where he played either the victim or the hapless, paradoxically powerless bully. No other comedians of the time come close to the wraithlike sociopath Groucho portrays in the Marx Brothers' best films.

Still, on rare occasions, Groucho's Archimedean outsiderness appears in a specific social context that tethers it to a moral framework. In *Monkey Business*, "Big Joe" Helton, a ruthless gangster, is the only figure who gets routinely insulted and deceived by Groucho's character, yet he laughs sympathetically, no matter what outrage Groucho visits upon him. He is, in fact, the only figure of wealth and power to enjoy Groucho's hostility in any of the Marx Brothers' films. Even more surprising, he is the one high-status figure—despite being a criminal—for whom the Brothers gladly go to work, risking their lives to save his daughter from another gangster who has abducted her.

The implication is clear. The nameless stowaways that the Brothers play in the film share Helton's moral nature. Like him, they operate on the margins of society. Like him, they are outlaws, lawbreakers, who will resort to mendacity and violence when they have to. This would have struck a sympathetic chord in many of their audiences at the time. The year *Monkey Business* came out, 1931, was the same year as the release of two gangster films, *Little Caesar* and *Public Enemy*, that virtually turned gangsters into romantic heroes for Depression-era moviegoers. Groucho's hostility toward respectable wealth and high society was one variation on the gangster's hostility toward the respectable society that had betrayed him and driven him into a life of crime. By the end of *Monkey Business*, after the Brothers violently vanquish Big Joe's rival, Big Joe himself stands as the movie's sole representative of privilege, respectability, and wealth.

The only other time in the Marx Brothers' films when Groucho, Harpo, and Chico seem to be making an explicit social comment is during the dance scene in *A Day at the Races*. Often dismissed as just another instance of Hollywood racism, the scene is, on the contrary, as strong a statement of racial equality as you can find in the world of Hollywood film.

Pursued by the forces of capital and law and order—dishonest businessmen abetted by a corrupt sheriff and his men—who are bent on taking over Standish Sanitarium, the Brothers flee into the black section of town, a collection of shanties and shacks.

The transition to the lavish spectacle of blacks dancing lays the groundwork for the scene's eventual import. We go from the two white lovers—Thalberg's insistence on a boy-girl romance as subplot—crooning to each other to Harpo suddenly appearing to serenade them on a piccolo. Then Harpo proceeds to march with a hop and a lilt into the black neighborhood. A group of black children follow him as his melody acquires a jazz rhythm. He encounters a group of black teenagers who point to him, singing, "Who dat man?" They answer their own question: "He's Gabriel!"—a recurrent archangelic figure in Negro spirituals.

Soon the crowd of boys and Harpo hear plaintive singing coming from inside a shanty. Slowly, with a kind of awestruck reverence, Harpo leads the boys up to the house and looks in the window. We see a large black family going about its daily life: a woman rolls dough as two other women play checkers and a man stands before the mirror brushing his hair, buttoning the top button on his shirt, and putting on his hat. The scene's social and domestic harmony is a dramatic contrast to the greed-driven menace of the white men pursuing the Brothers, which has been the main action of the movie so far.

The people in the house notice Harpo, hail him as Gabriel, and leave the house, joining the crowd of boys and following him into a clearing between shanties. They all come upon another shanty, where inside black people are playing various instruments, and they too proclaim Harpo to be Gabriel and pour outside. By now, the entire black part of town is dancing and singing behind the dancing, piccolo-playing Harpo. They dance into a large barn, back to the white lovers, who sing, somewhat blandly, "Tomorrow is another day." Harpo then swings back to a black dancer who sings "Tomorrow is another day" with a bounce and a soulfulness lacking in the white version. Then Harpo gestures to a black woman, who steps out from the crowd and launches into a beautiful version of "All God's Chillun Got Wings":

All God's chillun got rhythm
All God's chillun got swing
Maybe haven't got money
Maybe haven't got shoes
All God's chillun got rhythm
For to push away the blues
Yeah!

All God's chillun got trouble
Trouble don't mean a thing . . .

The reference to Eugene O'Neill's sensationally controversial drama of several years before is deliberate and purposeful. That play is about an interracial marriage in which a white woman viciously turns on her black husband, screaming "Nigger!" in one of the play's climactic scenes. (And perhaps, after mercilessly parodying O'Neill's *Strange Interlude* a few years earlier, in *Animal Crackers*, the Brothers wanted to make amends.)

The black singer, played by Ivie Anderson, leads the troupe into a dance routine that arrives as yet another jolt in the world of the movie. Harpo comes back into the dance, once again dancing at the head of a black crowd, as he holds a pitchfork, looking like the devil himself. At that very moment, the music shifts, briefly, into John Philip Sousa's "Stars and Stripes Forever," as though flipping the bird to the national self-image.

This is what America should look like, the film implies. In the New Testament, Gabriel announces the appearance of God on earth. That is why Gabriel plays such an important role in Negro spirituals, which call for the day when justice will bring dignity and peace. Here, Harpo, the childlike, traumatized Jewish mute, makes the annunciation. The figure of God appears to be realized through the black dancers themselves. That is why Harpo makes his reverential, awestruck face when he first sees them.

Against the greed, dirty-dealing, and general unhappiness of the powers ranged against the Brothers—exemplified by the white uniforms and environment of the sanitarium, a refuge for rich, mentally exhausted white people—the black dancers show a self-surrender, esthetic discipline, and inexhaustible joy in their dancing. When the bad guys finally get to the barn, the Brothers hide under a wagon and smear black axle grease over their faces, then mix into the crowd and do a brief bit of blackface dancing. Blackface was an esthetically and morally complicated vaudeville convention, but here the solidarity between Jews and blacks is the only note that's struck. Groucho and his brothers are outlaws, outcasts, and singular reproaches to white society's injustices and hypocrisies. That makes them one with blacks. A Day *of* the Races is more like it.

Decades later, on *Firing Line* in 1967, William F. Buckley

Jr. tells a bristling Groucho that he has no problem with whites continuing to perform in blackface, insisting that context is everything and that well-intentioned whites doing the old minstrel routine would be morally unobjectionable. "I wouldn't object to a Negro troupe doing a minstrel show," Groucho tells him, with some annoyance. "But today I would object to a white troupe doing it." The veteran survivor of vaudeville's depredations could not forget what it was like to be consigned to the bottom of society, talent and intelligence be damned.

Stirring as the dance scene in *A Day at the Races* is, and despite Groucho's sympathy for black people, the episode is the only instance in the Marx Brothers' films where the moral referents, as in most comedy, are clear. Elsewhere the Brothers exist beyond comedy's and satire's usual navigational points of little guy versus big guy, outsider versus insider. Groucho's relentless persecution of Margaret Dumont's wealthy and privileged characters—he loved startling and humiliating her with practical jokes offscreen as well—has no foundation in any kind of morality. Dumont's characters may be pompous, stuffy, and somewhat pretentious, but they are harmless and often kind.

Groucho's eventual persona grew out of stock figures in vaudeville, especially the figures of the cranky professor and the inflated financier. But when you try to come up with the closest precedent to the character Groucho gradually developed, and which found its fullest expression on the screen, your thought turns away from other comics and comedians. You find yourself in American literature.

Groucho could hardly be said to have borrowed anything at all from Mark Twain or Herman Melville. But his so-called comedy—a relentless abrasiveness contained within the form of humor—does the backstroke in the dark stream that courses through the work of both authors.

In the small, rural Arkansas town that Huck Finn and Jim visit, Huck witnesses a shooting. A certain Colonel Sherburn has just killed another man in cold blood. The victim was the town drunk, Boggs, who for many years rode up and down the town's main street screaming abusive accusations and threatening to kill people. On the day Huck encounters him, Boggs threatens the dignified and elegantly dressed Sherburn, who warns the man that if he does not stop menacing him, Sherburn will shoot him dead at one o'clock in the afternoon. Though Boggs is obviously a harmless, alcoholic fantasist, Sherburn cuts him down at the appointed hour. A crowd appears and proceeds to become a lynch mob, but Sherburn eloquently and with great dignity excoriates them, speaking of the cowardice of crowds and of the average man. The crowd slinks away, ashamed. Immediately after the incident, Huck visits a circus that has come to town, where he watches a seemingly drunken clown come riding in on a horse just like Boggs, and then stand up on the horse with the dignity and elegance of Colonel Sherburn.

The reader is left flailing amid the disturbing questions the episode raises. Did Sherburn kill the harmless Boggs because he lacked the imagination to realize that Boggs was merely faking; or did he kill him out of sheer malice? Where does the greater shock lie, in Boggs's unexpected fate or in Sherburn's unexpected reaction? Like the clown who is simultaneously Boggs and Sherburn—he is simultaneously, you might say, the insulting Groucho and the respectable figures Groucho insults—America is, all at once, innocent and guilty, harmless and malicious.

Twain's hybrid clown is present in Harpo's hybrid nature of victim and bully, and especially in Groucho's verbal enactment of the same double nature. Nearly all the characters Groucho played on film are morally ambiguous.

Mr. Hammer is an underdog trying to save his hotel, but he is also a skinflint and a liar bent on not paying his employees. Captain Spaulding, the outrageous antiestablishment figure, is out to exploit Mrs. Rittenhouse. The plucky stowaway Groucho plays in *Monkey Business* is perfectly comfortable working for Big Joe Helton, a ruthless gangster. Professor Wagstaff admirably outrages the stuffed-shirt atmosphere of Huxley College, even as he presides over Harpo's book burning, makes a mockery of higher education, insults his son, and pursues his son's girlfriend. Driftwood, though sympathetic to Tomasso, tries to represent Lassparri, knowing full well that the tenor has viciously beat his servant; Hackenbush, the savior of Standish Sanitarium, is an out-and-out medical fraud who encourages his patron, Mrs. Upjohn, to take a horse pill and continually lies to her about her true medical condition. There was nothing in comedy up to that point that even approximates Groucho's morally ambiguous nature. The moral ambiguity of Groucho's comedy is how he made war on comedy.

Along with Sherburn, there is another marginal figure in American literature, a character of Archimedean proportions. He is Bartleby, in Melville's great and haunting tale "Bartleby the Scrivener." Working as a clerk in a law firm, Bartleby eventually stops fulfilling his duties. "I would prefer not to," he says when asked to perform the tasks for which he is being paid. Eventually his refusal to abide by even the most elementary social requirements spells his gradual doom. He declines into penury, illness, and death.

Of course Groucho and his brothers never enact such a depressing picture of life. But in their determined occupation of a space beyond society, especially in Groucho's case, they are enacting what you might call the bright side of Melville's vexing character. It is difficult to accept what Melville meant by the story, which is that self-destruction is one fulfillment of free will. The benevolent attorney who tries to save Bartleby, risking his reputation and his sanity, also, like Bartleby, defies the law of self-preservation. Anyone, it seems, who allows himself to form any type of sympathetic bond with Bartleby will join him in his enigmatic downward spiral.

"I would prefer not to" could well serve as Groucho's credo; it is one step away from "Whatever it is, I'm against it." His characters would prefer not to look other characters in the eye when they talk to them. They would prefer not to communicate except through slashing, insulting non sequiturs, double entendres, and puns. They would prefer to run away from whoever approaches them. They would prefer not to work for a living. They would prefer to make sly references to sex while thwarting themselves whenever they are about to succeed at seduction. They would prefer not to even interact with the characters inhabited by Chico and Harpo. In their radical fulfillment of free will, Groucho's characters vanquish the world around them, and then proceed to obstruct themselves.

The personas of Chaplin, Keaton, Lloyd, Laurel and Hardy, Fields exist organically, within plots. Their fates are affected by the characters around them, with whom they are able to communicate. But even in their post-Paramount movies, which are all structured by at least a flimsy plot, the Marx Brothers operate in an autonomous world, and within that, each brother inhabits a further autonomous world. Yet you can sit through several of their films without laughing at all.

Chaplin eating his shoe in *The Gold Rush* makes you laugh. Hardy asking Laurel to tell him what time it is when Laurel is holding a glass of water, hoping to make him turn his hand and spill the water on himself, makes you laugh when you discover Laurel is wearing his watch with the face on the inside of his wrist and thus spills the water on Hardy. W. C. Fields makes you laugh when he says, in *Never Give a Sucker an Even Break*, "I was in love with a beautiful blonde once. . . . She drove me to drink. That's the one thing I am indebted to her for."

But Groucho's perpetually thwarted reason, at the hands

of Chico and Harpo, and his invective have a different effect. They bring you to a stasis that amounts to a silence. If Groucho's characters often serve to shift the action from Harpo's pantomime into social patter, then Harpo performs a complementary service. He completes Groucho's language as it melts into a critical mass of insult and frustration by consummating its inner purpose: the creation of a space where not a sound, especially not that of human speech, is heard.

Granted, humor is one of the most subjective human experiences, right up there with romantic love. But I submit that the one quality all Jewish humor shares is that the humor is only one degree removed from what is most serious, grave, profound, or tragic in life. The stasis and silence Groucho brings us to doesn't only make war on comedy by undermining the comedian's main objective, which is to make the audience laugh. It brings us to the point where humor blurs into its opposite. It makes the outsider comic an outsider even to comedy by making comedy philosophical.

In his novel *Watt*, Samuel Beckett, an ardent fan of the Marx Brothers, posits three types of laughter: "the bitter laugh [that] laughs at that which is not good, it is the ethical laugh"; "the hollow laugh [that] laughs at that which is not true, it is the intellectual laugh." For the first of these laughs, Beckett is perhaps thinking of comic playwrights like Aristophanes and Moliere; for the second, the Shakespeare of *Twelfth Night*, for example. Laughing at that which is not good or true is not so crisply identifiable in popular comedy.

The third laugh, however, is recognizable. It is, Beckett writes, "the mirthless laugh . . . the laugh of laughs, the risus purus, the laugh laughing at the laugh, the beholding, the saluting of the highest joke, in a word the laugh that laughs—silence please—at that which is unhappy." It is, you might say, the comedy of existence itself.

There are plenty of funny moments in the Marx Brothers' work, and in Groucho's verbal performances. When the Brothers, pretending to be doctors in *A Day at the Races*, evade demands that they prove their credentials by examining a patient, they say: "We don't do pulse work." Professor Wagstaff's biology lecture has its hilarious moments. But on the whole, Groucho's badinage, Chico's non sequiturs, seemingly unwitting puns, and malapropisms no longer work as comedy, if they ever did with any type of regularity.

Instead the Brothers, and especially Groucho, hold you with the spectacle of people saying whatever they think, and doing whatever they feel like doing. Since both laughter and shocking social behavior depend on surprise, on the unexpected, the Marx Brothers' outrages have the form of comedy but not the content. They drive laughter away from performing its function of relief, of catharsis. They are saying: Social life is too rigid, ritualistic, and mindless to be merely the butt of a joke. It has to be the object of unremitting hostility and antisocial behavior. Laughter, after all, is an expression of gregariousness, of sociableness, and gregariousness is the one quality all cultures share. In the world of Groucho, though, gregariousness is out of the question. All social relations are unbearable, and since laughter is a social expression, it becomes intolerable.

The reason social relations are portrayed as unbearable in the Brothers' movies is that they always betray the individual. Life taught them that. You get thrown out the window. You catch gonorrhea from your first sexual experience. You lose money and become obsessed with winning it back. Your character, added to reality, leads you to unhappiness. And so you create the mirthless laugh: "That shows a nice spirit."

From the Broadway show, *I'll Say She Is!:*

> CHICO: The garbage man is here.
> GROUCHO: Well, tell him we don't want any.

Not funny, but a response as unexpected as a joke and more true than a joke could ever be about what the world brings to your doorstep, and about what people will try to sell you or get you to accept.

From *A Day at the Races:*

> MAN: Are you a man or a mouse?
>
> GROUCHO: Put a piece of cheese on the floor and you'll find out.

A revelation of character that no one would make about himself except in the context of humor, but what makes this more memorable than a joke is that its level of seriousness overwhelms its short-lived humor. It is a revelation about a man's character, and about one of life's bitter truths: Courage falters before animal nature's elemental demand: to preserve yourself.

As Groucho puts it in *Animal Crackers*, "Well, all the jokes can't be good. You've got to expect that once in a while." Especially when you are mocking the very act of making people laugh.

The reason Beckett lifted the hat-switching scene right out of *Duck Soup* for *Waiting for Godot* could well be that he understood that the Marx Brothers were after the same risus purus, as he put it, as he was. But the differences between the two scenes are telling. In *Godot*, the discovery of a new hat and the subsequent confusion over whose hat belongs to whom, as Vladimir and Estragon try the new hat on as well as trying on each other's hat, rises to a metaphysical pathos and tenderness. There is an ineffable sweetness to finding the right hat, which feels comforting and good on your head, protects your brain, and expresses who you are as a particular human being. In *Duck Soup*, the confusion that ensues when Chico and Harpo, who are persecuting the poor, harmless lemonade vendor, snatch his hat off his head is brutal and inhumane. Here there is no comfort, protection, secure feeling of identity. There are only attacking and defending egos that obliterate the individuality conferred by a hat. A point about human existence is being made, within the convention of slapstick comedy.

Pardon me for bringing up Nietzsche, not known for side-splitting stand-up routines, but he once quipped that "jokes are epigrams on the death of feelings." Groucho's jokes are predicated on the death of feeling. Reducing language to sounds, intellectual life to disorder, and emotional life to physical gestures, Groucho's and his brothers' routines exist on the threshold of first and last things—that is to say, philosophy.

Groucho, who was well aware of inflated intellectual critiques of his and his brothers' work—by Artaud, for example—often said that all they were ever trying to do was to make people laugh. That's true, of course. He was a consummate performer, and if his words aren't funny on the page, that is sometimes because they are not accompanied by his impeccable sense of timing, his genius for gesture, and that raspy, world-weary voice. But even with all that, his humor often has the effect of racing past laughter itself to an exhaustion with the world of appearances. Just because Groucho wanted merely to entertain doesn't mean that he didn't come up with something that went beyond entertainment. He fulfilled Jewish humor's quintessential tendency. He made it philosophical.

You think that's funny? Please hear me out. Saul Bellow, The Serious Jewish Writer, once said that he preferred what he called philosophical jokes. He once gave an example to an interviewer of one of his favorite instances of philosophical humor. It goes like this:

A young American tenor is making his debut at La Scala. He sings his showcase aria and the crowd cries "Ancora! Ancora!" (Encore! Encore!) So he sings it again. Once more, the crowd erupts into loud shouts of "Ancora! Ancora!" The tenor takes a deep breath and performs the aria for a third time. "Ancora! Ancora!" shouts the crowd. The young singer holds up his hands. "Thank you," he says. "Thank you from the bottom of my heart. You have no idea how much this means to me," he says, his voice trembling. "I was raised by my mother, who was a laundress in Kansas City. She worked her fingers to the bone, scrimped and saved, and sent me to study music at Juilliard in New York. All my life I've dreamed of this moment. I am so moved and so grateful to you for your response. Thank you. Thank you. But the orchestra is waiting, the other singers are waiting, and the opera has to go on. Please let us continue." With that, he takes a step back to allow the opera to proceed, and a voice comes from the back of the hall: "Oh no! You gonna sing this till you get it right!"

Bellow no doubt loved the joke because it enacts the hard truth that our conception of ourselves is rarely the same as the world's perception of us, a cognitive pratfall that leads to both comic and tragic consequences. The La Scala joke exists on the famously imperceptible line between laughter and tears. You can easily imagine it as the occasion for a heartrending short story. It is a good example of Beckett's "mirthless laugh." The joke about the young tenor exists at the expense of the dignity of the young man, whose life story possesses such poignancy. If you laugh at that joke, you are also laughing at the fact that in human existence the humiliation of a pure-hearted young man is often the stuff of a joke. You are laughing at laughter itself. The same dynamic applies to Groucho's famous quip: "He may look like an idiot and talk like an idiot but don't let that fool you. He really is an idiot." You are laughing—if you do laugh—partly at the very fact that the humiliation of another person is the occasion for laughter.

One conventional explanation of why we laugh at jokes is that a joke makes us feel superior to clueless or—especially in the case of slapstick—hapless people. A joke confers on us superiority and a sense of power. Perhaps this is true, to a great extent. But there is a small class of jokes, like the one about the American tenor, to which this principle does not apply. I call these there-but-for-the-grace-of-God-go-I jokes. They plunge us into the situation of the joke's protagonist, and send through us waves of both pleasure and pain.

There-but-for-the-grace-of-God jokes are at the pinnacle of the philosophical joke category. And at the zenith of this category itself are the jokes in which the protagonist of the joke and the teller of the joke are, maybe, the same person. Groucho, who—along with his brothers—so completely fused his own life and personality with his comic persona, had this type of joke inscribed in his DNA.

The mirror scene in *Duck Soup* is widely and deservedly regarded as one of the greatest pantomimes ever created. In flight from a pursuer, Harpo, dressed in nightgown and cap, mistakes a large wall mirror for empty space, attempts to jump through it, and ends up destroying the mirror. Groucho, dressed in identical nightgown and cap, runs upstairs looking for the source of all the noise. As he walks past the space where the mirror used to be, not realizing that the mirror is no longer there, he notices his reflection. This is none other than Harpo, who has decided to pretend to be Groucho's image in the mirror. Harpo seems obsessed with Groucho's shadow, and with his image.

The scene progresses, becoming ever more absurd and outrageous, until we see Groucho make a motion that Harpo fakes but doesn't imitate. We are not sure whether Groucho also sees the mistake; in any case, he keeps going, trying to outwit his reflection because he seems to think something is up. The turning point comes when Harpo drops a hat he is now holding in his hand, and Groucho bends to pick it up, handing it back to Harpo. This doesn't stop Groucho, however. He continues trying to outfox Harpo, even after he has proved, beyond the shadow of a doubt, that it is Harpo he sees in the mirror, not himself.

Relief at not being himself, suspicion of his own image, a shared identity with Harpo, a characteristic contempt for appearances—"He may look like an idiot and talk like an idiot but don't let that fool you. He really is an idiot"—so much that is unique to Groucho and the Marx Brothers is going on in this scene. It is the visual equivalent, and all the more remarkable for that, of Groucho's and Chico's nonsense puns and non sequiturs. Groucho stooping to pick up Harpo's hat echoes perhaps his most famous bit of prose–Peasie Weasie: "One morning I shot an elephant in my pajamas. How he got in my pajamas, I don't know." What Groucho does to the phrase "in my pajamas" is the same as what he does to the idea of a mirror image. He turns what we know about the phrase's meaning, and the mirror's function, inside out.

But the most striking experience the mirror scene leaves you with is that of not knowing who is looking at whom. Before Groucho is trying to trick Harpo into revealing himself, he seems to be trying to outwit his own reflection. He seems to want to see himself as other people see him when he is not looking. By the time he reaches through the space that is serving as a mirror to pick up Harpo's hat, he has become both the teller of the joke, and the joke itself.

It would be like someone telling the joke about the American tenor who knows full well that he is, at that very moment, living through the same experience as the American tenor. Or as if the wife in the joke from Odessa were to say, "Ours is the best" when her husband's girlfriend walks by, not as the unaware protagonist of a joke, but as the one making an ironic joke herself, not at her own expense, but directed at people who would say exactly that in her situation.

These would be jokes that laugh at the convention itself of making people laugh. By having Groucho continue trying to outwit his reflection after he realizes it is someone else, the mirror scene is mocking its own comical pretense, even as it grows ever more comically absurd. Having used comedy to spew disdain for respectability, Groucho could not resist the impulse—the more respectable he became—to rain contempt down upon comedy.

Epilogue: Gone Today, Here Tomorrow

Keep warm.
—Charlie Chaplin saying good-bye to
Groucho at a party in 1972

With the exception of their brief reunion for *A Night in Casablanca* in 1946, the Marx Brothers broke up for good in 1941, during the filming of *The Big Store*. Groucho told a newspaper at the time, "When I say we're sick of the movies, I mean the people are about to get sick of us. By getting out now, we're just anticipating public demand." Groucho was an anxious man, and though he ended up outliving all his brothers except Zeppo, he spent his life waiting for the other shoe to drop. By the 1940s, his sense that the Brothers had outlived their originality was magnifying the frustration he already felt with the persona he had created.

Groucho's sense of the social and cultural atmosphere was

as keen as his comic timing. In 1941, a Gallup Poll asked people who their favorite fifteen comedians were. The Marx Brothers came in thirteenth, behind, among others, Red Skelton, Arthur Godfrey, Jimmy Durante, Fred Allen, Amos 'n' Andy, and Fibber McGee. Yet few people nowadays under the age of fifty would recognize these figures' names, let alone identify them as comedians. Even the more long-lived comics on the list—Bob Hope, Jack Benny, Danny Kaye—have nothing like the name recognition of the Marx Brothers, and of Groucho Marx above all.

Groucho's frankness, nonexistent in entertainment and public life until he and his brothers came along, is what has guaranteed his longevity. Even when you are watching his candor on film, it is as though you were experiencing it in a real situation. The routines might be outrageous and mad, but the fundamental social realities that they wrestle to the ground are all the more real for that. Groucho's professional resurrection on *You Bet Your Life* was the consummation of this capacity that Groucho had to knock down the wall between fiction and reality.

You Bet Your Life, in which contestants had to guess a secret word, started as a radio show on ABC in 1947. It did modestly well, and moved to CBS, a larger network, two years later. Finally, in 1950, the show made its television debut. It ran for eleven years.

There are still a few misconceptions about the show, the chief one recently reiterated in a 2014 biography of Bill Cosby by Mark Whitaker: that the quiz show was "rigged." This is both an overstatement and a distortion of the facts. In the wake of the sensational quiz show scandal involving Mark Van Doren in 1959, the FCC investigated *You Bet Your Life* and found nothing illegal or improper. What vexes some people who look back on it is the fact that it seemed spontaneous but often wasn't. Though Groucho did not meet with the contestants beforehand, he was made aware of themes that might surface in the broadcast. Comedy writers were brought in to come up with appropriate gags. Cue cards, invisible to home viewers and the studio audience, were also displayed to help Groucho bring off the appearance of being the supreme ad-libber he was touted as. The show wasn't rigged, because the contestants did not know what questions they would be asked, and Groucho didn't know what their answers would be. Rather, the entertainment segment of the show, Groucho's badinage with his guests, was often scripted. Yet he was still very much the champion ad-libber. His spontaneous quips and comebacks were legendary among the people involved in the show. As with the Marx Brothers' films, no one knows to what extent Groucho was involved in the lines he spoke. The only certainty was that he frequently improvised his own jokes.

You Bet Your Life solidified Groucho's reputation and brought him to a level way beyond his comedic contemporaries. This development was accompanied by a considerable amount of irony. Groucho began to be celebrated as the nonconformist doing battle with wealth, privilege, and established authority at the same moment that he was being turned into a comfortable commodity.

Groucho was well aware of the danger of the persona he had created becoming a caricature of itself. After *You Bet Your Life* moved to television, the producers asked him to appear in his frock coat, bushy eyebrows, and mustache made of greasepaint. "The hell I will," he told them. "That character's dead. I'll never go into that again." Instead he appeared on the show with real spectacles, a real mustache, and an ordinary suit and bowtie. The cigar remained, but now it was a cigar, and not merely a prop.

The newly tricked-out seasoned outsider formed an instant bond with his audience. At a time of fear and paranoia—the House Un-American Activities Committee held its first hearings on communism's influence in Hollywood the same month *You Bet Your Life* made its radio debut—Groucho's insolence toward his guests, from clerks to generals, was a welcome relief. (Groucho himself succumbed to pressure and dropped the show's music director when the latter took the Fifth Amendment during an appearance before HUAC. He was scared, like nearly everyone else.)

At the same time, *You Bet Your Life* gave robust expression to the new egalitarianism the Second World War had created. As men of all races and religions and from all classes fought side by side, society began to level out. Women from all backgrounds and walks of life working together in factories where war materiel was being made had the same social effect. On *You Bet Your Life*, Groucho no longer took the poo-bahs as his exclusive target. Landing on the egos of big shots as well as small businessmen, tradespeople, and housewives, his insults expressed the new tenor of American democracy. Their universal hostility had a Jacksonian quality to it.

Groucho scholars often talk about this new, universal Groucho as being a softening of the old, hard misanthropic character, but the opposite is the case. The quiz show format, in which he insulted a broad cross-section of Americans, exposed for the first time the personal roots of Groucho's professional entertainer's shtick. It seems that all along, he was for real. He wasn't just making stuff up. He actually felt like that about other people. So even as the visibly aging Groucho made people feel comfortable about the invective, the veteran outsider, who was making a nonconformist tone available to the new mass audience created by television, was inventing a new confrontational public style.

Groucho's personality and his persona, for the first time, merged comfortably, definitively, in full public view. Nowadays we are used to a style of both popular and serious art in which fiction merges into autobiographical and documentary fact.

Groucho was, if not the sole pioneer of that style, certainly its most influential.

Comedy evolved into a whole new form during the years when *You Bet Your Life* was on the air. From 1947, when the show debuted on radio, to 1961, its final year on television, comedy passed through several distinct stages. They might all have grown out of the various levels of comedy on Groucho's show. In the late 1940s, stand-up came into its own with comedians like Henny Youngman, Shecky Greene, Don Rickles, and Jack Carter plying the one-liner style that Groucho had made famous in his films and still practiced on television. In the 1950s and 1960s, it was Groucho's confrontational brio that influenced comedians like Lenny Bruce and Dick Gregory. And the seemingly casual, conversational wit that Groucho perfected on the show surfaced in Mort Sahl's monologues, which had the same casual, conversational quality but lacked the brutal candor of Bruce and Gregory.

From that point on, Groucho's two streams of humor, the confrontational and the conversational, both assimilated by television and responsible for opening up television's borders, have influenced comedians to this day. Groucho's comic art is stamped all over the comedians who came to prominence in the 1970s and flourished for decades after that: Woody Allen, Bill Cosby, George Carlin, Richard Pryor, Robert Klein, et al.

You can see Groucho's influence on the comedy of Cosby, Carlin, and Klein as they transform *You Bet Your Life*'s discursive style into their own long anecdotes, which were half humor, half wisdom-talking. But Woody Allen is perhaps the figure most responsible for Groucho's persistence into posterity. He carried Groucho's influence forward both in his physical appearance and his intellectual style. Allen was what Lenny Bruce might have turned into had Bruce survived and gone into therapy. Whereas Bruce wholly assimilated Groucho's explicit style of insult, Allen appropriated Groucho's way of presenting himself in the worst possible light in order to unmask the follies of other people. In Allen's hands, Bruce's rage became a passive-aggressive, self-deprecating irony—with a heavy emphasis on the self-deprecation.

In this respect, Allen's misinterpretation of Groucho's resignation letter as the epitome of—especially Jewish—self-hatred is telling. As we have seen, Groucho's letter is the supreme example of how he abased himself in order to elevate himself. The letter of resignation is, contrary to Allen, the epitome of Jewish pride and self-confidence. In his act, however, Allen played up the self-hatred in order to put a more crowd-pleasing edge on his aggression. Even the oversized black-frame glasses that he wore were a devolution of Groucho's comedic self-presentation. Groucho's glasses signaled a cerebral assault on respectable society's fatuousness. Allen's glasses, often knocked slantwise by some bully, indicated the disintegration of intellect into debilitating neurosis and vulnerability. In debasing himself with a superior air, Groucho proclaimed his refusal to be a schlemiel. Allen's schlemielitude, if you will, made his mordant wit palatable to a mass audience.

Comedians from Sacha Baron Cohen, on his now-defunct *Da Ali G Show*, to—in various incarnations—Larry David, Jon Stewart, Stephen Colbert, and Bill Maher have reclaimed Groucho's harsh candor and fused his confrontational and his conversational styles. The entire country seems finally to be catching up with Groucho's stinging frankness as insolence toward authority becomes the hallmark style of digital culture. You can almost feel Groucho's influence like a brisk wind, both chilling and invigorating, as the general style of confrontation, exposure, and insult alternates between the humorous and the plain, unadulterated expression of spleen.

Yet though comedy and culture have gone around, behind, and through Groucho and his brothers, they have not passed beyond them. The reason is simple. It is summed up by Edgar in *King Lear*, the literary work Groucho once determinedly expounded to T. S. Eliot, in the play's final lines, the admonition to "speak what we feel, not what we ought to say." Groucho heeded that impulse for more than seventy years. In our moment, when truth-telling has become a collaborative enterprise with its own official boundaries, speaking what we feel and not what we ought to say, and doing it with idiosyncratic flair and individual commitment (not to say, compulsion), is still a quality that is both exceptionally rare—and all but impossible to assimilate.

A NOTE ON SOURCES

PERHAPS IT is in the nature of an icon to have all the human substantiality of a desert mirage, but there is very little critical literature about Groucho. Although in his own autobiography, pointedly titled *Groucho and Me*, Groucho gestures at the personality underneath the screen persona, several generations of commentators on him have concentrated mostly on the screen persona. Some of these books are written with diligence and love, but they rarely get beyond extended celebrations of the "beloved" comic. The greasepaint—not to mention the fake eyebrows and mustache—almost never comes off.

For such literature as does exist on Groucho, however, the aspiring critical biographer must be grateful. The keystone of Groucho studies is Wes Gehring's meticulous *The Marx Brothers: A Bio-Bibliography*, published in 1987. Gehring sifts dispassionately, and with a sharper critical eye than any other Marxian, through the literature on the Brothers, as well as through all the known facts of their lives, and delivers subtle judgments and interpretations of the interplay between their lives and their work. His book is a slim volume, suggestive rather than exhaustive, but it is rich with intelligent perceptions and connections.

In his 1950 *The Marx Brothers,* Kyle Crichton had the advantage of knowing the Brothers themselves, but he also suffers from the disadvantage of knowing the Brothers themselves. The book has some useful facts, and is animated by the charm of its intimacy with its subjects, but it remains a superficial account. (Gehring, while generous to the book, observes that the Marx Brothers owned the book's copyright.)

The first detailed biography of Groucho was Hector Arce's 1979 *Groucho*. Arce offers a more complete picture of the world inhabited by Groucho and his brothers, but as a close friend of Groucho, he was in no position to cultivate a critical distance from him. Still, even more than Crichton's book, Arce's life benefits from its living, breathing proximity to the book's subject; it is a delight to read. Martin Gardner's *The Marx Brothers: An Investigation of Their Films as Satirical Social Criticism* began life as a Ph.D. dissertation and, alas, does not rise above its admirable yet naïve premise of the brothers as conscientious social critics. Simon Louvish's *Monkey Business: The Lives and Legends of the Marx Brothers* is a refreshing attempt, written with engaging brio, to cut through all the Marx Brothers mythologizing, but it too succumbs to its subjects' larger-than-life aura, as well as floundering amid a sea of irrelevant facts and dubious connections.

The most vigorous effort to compose an actual life of Groucho—a real biography, as it were—is Stefan Kanfer's 2000 *Groucho: The Life and Times of Julius Henry Marx*. The subtitle implies that Kanfer is finally going to pierce the screen persona and get to the man himself, but for the most part he settles for a comprehensive account of the life's outward events—and gratifyingly so. The value of the book lies in its trove of facts, and in its synthesis of what was known about Julius Marx at the time with what Kanfer managed to discover. Unfortunately the book is occasionally marred by its casual relationship with factual accuracy. Joe Adamson's *Groucho, Harpo, Chico, and Sometimes Zeppo*, for all its almost vaudevillian playfulness, is much better at going beneath Groucho's persona by delving into his work. It is essentially a highly enjoyable and extended romp through the films' backstories, done in a sort of echo of Marxian style.

The tendency of some of Groucho's and his brothers' would-be biographers to write in what they consider Groucho's own style is both a tribute to the infectiousness of Groucho's idiom and a cautionary lesson in the blinding optics of iconicity. Some books, like *The Groucho Phile: An Illustrated Life*, are worthy sources precisely because they don't pretend to be anything more than scrapbooks or compendiums of Marxiana. By contrast, there is Charlotte Chandler's massive oral biography, *Hello, I Must Be Going: Groucho and His Friends*, about which the term *starstruck* is breathtakingly inadequate. Chandler seems to have spent years following around the octogenarian Groucho and recording every word or sound that emanated from him or from his famous friends. The result is reams of often diverting, evanescent gossip. On the other end of that spectrum is Richard Anobile's collaboration with Groucho, *The Marx Brothers Scrapbook*, another oral biography, but gimlet-eyed and seemingly impervious to celebrity. Its flouting of biographical decency and discretion is a morally ambiguous godsend.

Of course, the memoirs of Groucho and Harpo make for essential, if problematic, reading. The two men are both performers, and even their "candid" self-portraits become part of their performances. That is no less the case for Groucho's letters, nearly all of which were published in a single volume in 1967: some scholars believe not only that Groucho edited the letters before the volume was published but that he wrote a few new ones to fill out the collection. Still, there are important differences between Groucho's two memoirs—the second, *Memoirs of a Mangy Lover* almost wholly lacks the spontaneity of the first, *Groucho and Me*—and Harpo's autobiography *Harpo Speaks!* Desiring all his life to be taken seriously as a literary man, Groucho produced a self-conscious impersonation of a literary man. His personal stories come across as highly tuned shticks. Harpo, on the other hand, had no literary pretensions and, with the help of a professional writer,

Rowland Barber, projects an air of artless recollection. Both books have to be read above, beneath, and between the lines in order to serve as revelations of personality, which they ultimately are despite themselves.

An opposite dynamic is present in the recollections written by Marx family members. These books were written by the children of performers, and they are explicit about wounds inflicted and disappointments suffered. They are, you might say, *written* above, beneath, and between the lines. These memoirs also serve as revelations of the Marx Brothers' personalities, but they have to be read with a robust dose of skepticism and a healthy sense of proportion.

Finally, and most important, are the priceless films. Groucho and his brothers—especially Groucho—walked in front of a camera and, rather than leaving their true selves behind, became ever truer to themselves. His performances onscreen are Groucho's fullest disclosure of who he really was. They are the biographical gold.

BIBLIOGRAPHY

Adamson, Joe. *Groucho, Harpo, Chico, and Sometimes Zeppo*. New York: Simon and Schuster, 1973.

Arce, Hector. *Groucho*. New York: Putnam, 1979.

Arnason, Johann, Kurt A. Raaflub, and Peter Wagner, eds. *The Greek Polis and the Invention of Democracy: A Politico-Cultural Transformation and Its Interpretations*. Chichester, U.K.: Wiley Blackwell, 2013.

Auden, W. H. *Collected Poems*. New York: Vintage International, 1991.

Beckett, Samuel. *Watt*. New York: Grove, 1959.

Buber, Martin. *Ten Rungs: Hasidic Sayings*. New York: Schocken, 1947.

Burrows, Edwin G., and Mike Wallace. *Gotham: A History of New York City to 1898*. New York: Oxford University Press, 1998.

Chandler, Charlotte. *Hello, I Must Be Going: Groucho and His Friends*. Garden City, N.Y.: Doubleday, 1978.

Crichton, Kyle. *The Marx Brothers*. Garden City, N.Y.: Doubleday, 1950.

Freud, Sigmund. *Jokes and Their Relation to the Unconscious*. New York: Norton, 1960.

Gabler, Neal. *An Empire of Their Own: How the Jews Invented Hollywood*. New York: Crown, 1988.

Gardner, Martin Allen. *The Marx Brothers: An Investigation of Their Films as Satirical Social Criticism*. Jefferson, N.C.: McFarland, 2009.

Gehring, Wes D. *The Marx Brothers: A Bio-Bibliography*. Westport, Conn.: Greenwood, 1987.

Howe, Irving. *The World of Our Fathers*. New York: Harcourt Brace Jovanovich, 1976.

Howe, Irving, and Eliezer Greenberg. *A Treasury of Yiddish Stories*. New York: Compass, 1954.

Kanfer, Stefan. *Groucho: The Life and Times of Julius Henry Marx*. New York: Knopf, 2000.

Louvish, Simon: *Monkey Business: The Lives and Legends of the Marx Brothers*. New York: St. Martin's, 2000.

Marx, Arthur. *Life with Groucho*. New York: Simon and Schuster, 1954.

———. *My Life with Groucho*. Fort Lee, N.J.: Barricade, 1988.

———. *Son of Groucho*. New York: McKay, 1972.

Marx, Bill. *Son of Harpo Speaks*. New York: Applause Theater and Cinema Books, 2011.

Marx, Groucho. *Beds*. Indianapolis: Bobbs-Merrill, 1930.

———. *Groucho and Me*. New York: Da Capo, 1995.

———. *The Groucho Letters*. New York: Simon and Schuster, 1967.

———. *Groucho Marx and Other Short Stories and Tall Tales: Selected Writings of Groucho Marx*. Ed. Robert S. Bader. New York: Applause Theater and Cinema Books, 2011.

———. *The Groucho Phile: An Illustrated Life*. New York: Galahad, 1976.

———. *Love, Groucho: Letters from Groucho Marx to His Daughter Miriam*. Ed. Miriam Marx Allen. New York: Da Capo, 2002.

———. *Memoirs of a Mangy Lover*. New York: Da Capo, 1997.

Marx, Groucho, with Richard Anobile. *The Marx Brothers Scrapbook*. 1973; rpt. New York: Harper and Row, 1989.

Marx, Groucho, with Hector Arce. *The Secret Word Is Groucho*. New York: Putnam, 1976.

Marx, Harpo, with Rowland Barber. *Harpo Speaks!* Pompton Plains, N.J.: Limelight, 2010.

Marx, Maxine. *Growing Up with Chico*. Englewood Cliffs, N.J.: 1980.

Shakespeare, William. *King Lear*. New York: Signet Classics, 1963.

———. *Troilus and Cressida*. New York: Signet Classics, 1963.

Wisse, Ruth. *No Joke: Making Jewish Humor*. Princeton: Princeton University Press, 2013.

ACKNOWLEDGMENTS

I COULD not have written this book without the support of John Donatich, who published it, and Ileene Smith, who edited it. I am profoundly grateful to both of them, professionally and personally.

If there is, so to speak, something going on in this book, it is the laughter of my children, Julian and Harper, both of whom, in the course of my writing it, perfected Groucho's walk, in their strange, unforgettable, and separate ways. I love you, Julian. I love you, Harper.

To my wife, Christina Gillham, I can only say thanks for continuing to find the comedy in our own existence.

CREDITS

Richard Anobile and Groucho Marx, excerpts, from *The Marx Brothers Scrapbook*, copyright © 1973 by Darien House, Inc. Reprinted by permission of HarperCollins Publishers.

"Sext (Horae Canonicae: 3)," copyright © 1955 by W. H. Auden, renewed 1983 by The Estate of W. H. Auden; from *W. H. Auden Collected Poems* by W. H. Auden. Used by permission of Random House, an imprint and division of Random House LLC. All rights reserved.

Groucho Marx, excerpts, from *Groucho and Me*, copyright © 1995 by Perseus Books Group. Reprinted by permission of Perseus Books Group.

INDEX

Jewish Lives is a major series of interpretive biography designed to illuminate the imprint of Jewish figures upon literature, religion, philosophy, politics, cultural and economic life, and the arts and sciences. Subjects are paired with authors to elicit lively, deeply informed books that explore the range and depth of Jewish experience from antiquity through the present.

Jewish Lives is a partnership of Yale University Press and the Leon D. Black Foundation.

Ileene Smith is editorial director. Anita Shapira and Steven J. Zipperstein are series editors.

PUBLISHED TITLES INCLUDE:

Ben-Gurion: Father of Modern Israel, by Anita Shapira
Bernard Berenson: A Life in the Picture Trade, by Rachel Cohen
Sarah: The Life of Sarah Bernhardt, by Robert Gottlieb
Leonard Bernstein: An American Musician, by Allen Shawn
Léon Blum: Prime Minister, Socialist, Zionist, by Pierre Birnbaum
David: The Divided Heart, by David Wolpe
Moshe Dayan: Israel's Controversial Hero, by Mordechai Bar-On
Einstein: His Space and Times, by Steven Gimbel
Becoming Freud: The Making of a Psychoanalyst, by Adam Phillips
Emma Goldman: Revolution as a Way of Life, by Vivian Gornick
Hank Greenberg: The Hero Who Didn't Want to Be One, by Mark Kurlansky
Peggy Guggenheim: The Shock of the Modern, by Francine Prose
Lillian Hellman: An Imperious Life, by Dorothy Gallagher
Jabotinsky: A Life, by Hillel Halkin
Jacob: Unexpected Patriarch, by Yair Zakovitch
Franz Kafka: The Poet of Shame and Guilt, by Saul Friedländer
Rav Kook: Mystic in a Time of Revolution, by Yehudah Mirsky
Primo Levi: The Matter of a Life, by Berel Lang
Groucho Marx: The Comedy of Existence, by Lee Siegel
Moses Mendelssohn: Sage of Modernity, by Shmuel Feiner
Proust: The Future's Secret, by Benjamin Taylor
Walter Rathenau: Weimar's Fallen Statesman, by Shulamit Volkov
Mark Rothko: Toward the Light in the Chapel, by Annie Cohen-Solal

Solomon: The Lure of Wisdom, by Steven Weitzman
Leon Trotsky: A Revolutionary's Life, by Joshua Rubenstein

FORTHCOMING TITLES INCLUDE:

Rabbi Akiva, by Barry Holtz
Irving Berlin, by James Kaplan
Hayim Nahman Bialik, by Avner Holtzman
Louis Brandeis, by Jeffrey Rosen
Martin Buber, by Paul Mendes-Flohr
Benjamin Disraeli, by David Cesarani
Bob Dylan, by Ron Rosenbaum
George Gershwin, by Gary Giddins
Allen Ginsberg, by Edward Hirsch
Ben Hecht, by Adina Hoffman
Heinrich Heine, by Fritz Stern
Theodor Herzl, by Derek Penslar
Jesus, by Jack Miles
Karl Marx, by Shlomo Avineri
Moses, by Avivah Zornberg
J. Robert Oppenheimer, by David Rieff
Rabin, by Itamar Rabinovich
Jerome Robbins, by Wendy Lesser
Julius Rosenwald, by Hasia Diner
Jonas Salk, by David Margolick
Gershom Scholem, by David Biale
Steven Spielberg, by Molly Haskell
Barbra Streisand, by Neal Gabler
The Warner Brothers, by David Thomson
Ludwig Wittgenstein, by Anthony Gottlieb